THE PURPOSE PROMISE

THE PURPOSE PROMISE

The Purpose Promise organization was developed so that you, the reader, can gain the most out of the journey to find purpose and joy in your work. This journey was not designed to be done alone. There are many ways to engage the journey to reach your destination of purpose and joy-filled work.
Visit www.purposepromise.org to discover resources to walk you towards your purpose.

Praise for *The Purpose Promise*

"In *The Purpose Promise,* John McCarthy has created much more than just another insightful book on fulfillment at work. *The Purpose Promise* has real impact, with vulnerable lessons from John's own life, clear examples from those he has helped, and simple action steps for the reader. I have watched John in action over the years, capably guiding people to fulfilling career choices despite the myriad complexities of work life. I encourage everyone to read this book, because life is meant to be filled with purpose, and this book brings purpose to work life."

—CHUCK PROUDFIT

"*The Purpose Promise* was a true blessing to me during my almost nine months in job transition. The guidance contained in *The Purpose Promise* helped me to keep everything in perspective. It gave me clarity that helped me land a career of purpose."

—BRET MEYER

"When I first met with John, my purpose was to get help finding a new job. However, John had something more in mind. What I was lacking was not just a job I enjoyed, it was purpose in my professional life. Because of *The Purpose Promise*, I have much more than a new job; I have a career with purpose."

—JONATHAN LAMB

"I am grateful to John and the techniques he employed from *The Purpose Promise* that helped guide me as I navigated through a challenging, but exciting, transition time in my career. He was able to help me clear out some of the noise and focus on a path that best suited my unique skills with both my professional and personal goals."

—SUSAN FISHER

"Finding my life's purpose has proven to be very challenging. Working with John McCarthy and *The Purpose Promise* has provided a platform of discernment with simple processes and exercises that has allowed me to focus on my identification of true success. It empowered me to find a career aligned with my unique purpose!"

—BETH PESSELL

"The process defined in *The Purpose Promise* was essential to guide me through my career transition. The stories, analogies, and exercises in *The Purpose Promise* challenged me to examine my life and career in a unique way. The process enabled me to identify my unique success and target the job opportunities that meet my critical needs."

—DAVID MOSS

THE PURPOSE PROMISE

How to Find Purpose and Joy in Your Work

John McCarthy

franciscan
media
Cincinnati, Ohio

Cover design by LUCAS Art & Design—Jenison, MI
Book design by Mark Sullivan

Library of Congress Control Number: 2019951763

ISBN 978-1-63253-290-9

Published by Franciscan Media
28 W. Liberty St.
Cincinnati, OH 45202
www.FranciscanMedia.org

Printed in the United States of America.
Printed on acid-free paper.
19 20 21 22 23 5 4 3 2 1

To my grace-filled children
Bella, Mason, and Lydia.

• • •

Live life fearlessly as yourself,
pursuing only your unique view
of success and purpose!

Contents

Acknowledgments

I OFTEN REFER TO THE PROCESS OF writing *The Purpose Promise* as caring for my fourth child. It takes a village to raise a child, no doubt, and it also takes a community to compile a life-changing and interactive book. I am forever grateful for the humility, acts of service, and wisdom so many have gifted me during the journey of writing *The Purpose Promise*.

Thank you to those that have stood in the trenches patiently on this journey with me: my wife, Julie; my three kiddos; my extended family; and my wise sounding boards along the journey, including Dave Ping, Danise Distasi, Becky Robinson, Erin Kutcher, Josephine McKenrick, Jan Hamilton, Audrey Hensley, Dan Henry, David McPherson, Jesse Reeves, Janet Slater, and Camille Nuckols.

I have great men in my life. I'm grateful for my humble and pious father, John McCarthy. Your steadfast modeling of how to be a man has set the healthy boundaries for my journey in life. I also thank the many men who have discipled me. You know who you are, and I'm blessed by your encouragement to be a great husband, father, and friend.

I also thank my mother, Bev McCarthy, whose passion and zeal for life has inspired me to have the courage to move mountains.

I am grateful to the many devout messengers of Christ that impart wisdom upon my journey. I am richly blessed by the life work of Bishop Robert Barron, Bill and Eric Johnson, Kris Vallotton, Todd White, Matthew Kelly, Ed Silvoso, and many other great teachers of truth. Thank you for your courage to carry the application of the Kingdom that God has revealed to you!

Above all, I give all the glory to God for the journey he has set before me. His grace and mercy are sufficient. Through the intimate and enjoyable relationship with my Creator, God, I have gained all the direction needed to walk with him into Purpose, Freedom, and Joy. Thank you!

Part One: How Did We Get Here?

chapter ONE

Life Lessons from the Rainforest

I AWOKE IN A PANIC TO THE SOUND of monkeys clamoring instead of an alarm clock. It was a hot, sticky morning in Costa Rica. I hadn't gotten much sleep the night before. The house was designed to let the dripping rainforest air in rather than keep its exotic and potentially dangerous wildlife out. The cockroaches in Costa Rica seemed like something out of a Marvel comic. Even scarier predators were no doubt lurking just outside my open window.

As I rose in the morning, I took inventory of my body. There were a few bug bites but nothing that would keep me from the day ahead. It was an exhilarating morning. The smells of the jungle were fresh and vivid. Each breath was an intoxicating experience. The color spectrum of the scenery rivaled a Crayola box. I marveled at the toucans gliding from one tree to the next. Until that day, the only toucan I'd known was on a cereal box

Suddenly the intensity of the unfamiliar setting became familiar. My sister, Kristin, squealed with joy. I greeted her with a long, familiar hug. She and her husband, Joshua, were building a Costa Rican retreat center and were no strangers to the fears and raptures of newcomers adjusting to rainforest living. Joshua picked up two machetes and handed me one. He had me step into a pair of knee-high rubber boots and explained that the poisonous snakes had no interest in biting me unless I stepped on them—so I should watch my step. He told Kristin we would be "back in a few" with breakfast for all.

I have always been adaptable, but this was a whole new level of adventure. My heightened emotions were a mix of fear and excitement, but I pretended that I had it together. I'm sure the mask of false confidence was no surprise to Joshua, but his demeanor was gentle and nonjudgmental. Following his lead was easy. He taught me how to knock coconuts off trees and use my machete to open them. He showed me which trees to harvest from and how to choose the ripe fruit. He taught me where the best avocado trees were and got me excited about the freshness of the food we would eat. He helped me feel at home in this new place.

In the rainforest, life is amplified and abundant. The level of amplification can be uncomfortable. If you focus on this discomfort, you can become overwhelmed by fear and feel ill-equipped. You may have a rotten experience, and worse, miss the beauty of life around you. Changing your perspective and embracing your fears will lead to a more powerful you.

The Costa Rica rainforest proved to be the ideal retreat for me at this point in my life. Retreats have always helped me gain clarity in my life. Most of the pivotal decisions I've made took root while I was retreating from my daily grind. I knew this was not going to be a typical vacation, but I could have never imagined the transformation I would encounter.

As I embraced the jungle adventure, I knew I was there for a purpose. My life path was not fulfilling. I set out to change my perspective, and in doing so, I uncovered new dreams. Those dreams set me on a path to help others on a journey to unlock their own purpose and dreams. While your journey may not involve poisonous snakes, vivid scenery, or foraging for food in the jungle, it will bring you to your best life.

The lack of clarity about how to live in the jungle brought me to profound vulnerability and fear. I needed great guides—Kristin and Joshua—to help me find the courage to overcome the conditions. Without them, I would have been lost and unable to navigate the dangerous terrain. Their expertise and wisdom were the catalyst that transformed my career path.

Today, over a decade after my Costa Rica discovery, I am living out my career purpose: helping seekers who are unhappy in their career paths. Maybe you are feeling lost and vulnerable on your quest for purpose, paralyzed by navigating the unchartered jungle ahead. Confronting this reality is a daring adventure, and I'm excited to walk with you toward a new, more fulfilling path.

The exercises in this book will lead you on a remarkable journey toward greater self-discovery and a path of purpose and joy. As your guide, I will walk with you through fear, vulnerability, and exciting discoveries. If you're interested in richer possibilities for your work, a more profound sense of purpose, and a more joy-filled life, read on!

chapter TWO

Life, Liberty, and Pursuit of Happiness

I GREW UP IN A LOVING, UPPER-CLASS home with great opportunity and the privilege of education. My goals were all about obtaining the conventional American Dream. After receiving my undergraduate degree, I joined a small recruiting firm that placed restaurant managers in new careers. It was a valuable start to my career and I succeeded at plucking disengaged restaurant managers out of their stalled jobs with the promise that the grass was greener in another restaurant.

At first, my new career path seemed to align with my value of helping others develop their livelihoods. But as I grew in the business and placed more managers in new management roles, I began to get discouraged. Often, I would work to help staff a restaurant's managerial team only to have the people I placed call me back in less than a year to see if they could get a better career in a new setting. I would ask why they weren't fulfilled at the current organization and hear a variety of reasons why their employers weren't ideal fits.

As I developed more in-depth relationships with clients, I began to hear more about how they had arrived at the positions in which they found themselves. Very few had wanted to become restaurant managers. Most had backed into their positions through serving or cooking jobs in high school. They were asked to become supervisors, a position that offered a bit of a pay increase and a chance to become a manager. Most of the managers who came to me seeking new roles in the restaurant industry didn't last long in their jobs. In turn, their organizations didn't expect the managers they were hiring to be with them for more than a year or two. It was a vicious cycle.

What I was doing wasn't leading to lasting fulfillment for those I was serving or fulfilling the desires that got me started in my line of work. I was increasingly unhappy knowing that the "life change" I was providing was temporary at best. I wanted to address the deep-rooted problem that led to what I called the treadmill of disengagement.

The Treadmill of Disengagement

I have always enjoyed exercise, especially when I am chasing after a ball or aiming for something I can hit. However, life's demands began to limit my time to exercise. I started running to get the most exercise out of the time I had. In the winter when it was too cold to run outside, I would go into the gym and get on a treadmill. It wasn't enjoyable, and the scenery was dull. It met my exercise needs, but I didn't get the same joy as when I was outside. The treadmill was a poor substitute for what I loved about exercise. I lacked passion for exercising on a treadmill. I had the discipline to do it, but I was less engaged because it wasn't a joyful experience.

Work was the same experience for most of the job seekers I was helping. They were running in place and so bored with their work environments that they would periodically jump onto another treadmill only to find it equally unfulfilling. The whole cycle produces ever-increasing levels of disengagement. Now that I help career seekers from many different industries, I can conclude that the treadmill of disengagement exists in every sector of every industry.

So how do we break this cycle? How do people find careers that keep them engaged and progressing toward a more profound life purpose that will fulfill their dreams? These are the questions that keep me up at night.

Most career seekers lack a strategic process to gain the self-awareness necessary to define and achieve a career of purpose. Work should be one of the best and most fulfilling parts of our lives, but a lack of self-awareness has fueled the treadmill of disengagement in our workforce.

Workplace statisticians agree that about 75 percent of the American workforce is disengaged in their work. That's a pretty startling statistic. This disengagement has a profound negative effect on individuals, families, and society at large. The effect on our country and our productivity is nothing short of catastrophic!

Smart employers spend significant time, energy, and money cultivating a culture of engagement. By caring about their workers, they hope to avoid the much higher costs of lost time, energy, and money caused by high turnover. Organizations focused on high engagement and retention realize that the employer-employee relationship is like a marriage—the better you understand and satisfy each other's needs, the happier everyone will be!

On the other hand, running on the treadmill of disengagement is like being in a loveless marriage. It generates frustration and bitterness for everyone involved. It doesn't matter how many times you remarry, as long as you're on the treadmill of disengagement, it can't get better. Career seekers and employers need to understand that work satisfaction is a two-way street.

When you are not engaged, you will not be happy with your job. When you are not happy in your job, it has a profound impact on all other aspects of your life. I regularly speak with people whose home lives are adversely affected by their unhappiness in their work lives. If you are not happy and engaged in your work, you will feel burdened by it.

Work should not be a burden. We were created to work. Doing so creates purpose. Life lacks meaning when we do not work with purpose. This lack of meaning will rob you of joy. To be released from this burden, you must invest in knowing yourself. You were made for a unique purpose. You will only find that purpose through self-awareness. It will be helpful to have a logical process to uncover your career purpose. This process will free you from your burden so you can dream again according to how you were created to work. It is time to start to view your career decisions with more diligence.

Liberty and Happiness

The third day of my Costa Rican retreat was a game changer for my life. Up to this point in my career, I had achieved success, according to the world's standards. It was not until I stopped, retreated, and examined my life that I realized the world's expectations of success burdened me. I was chasing after a mirage that carried me away from purposeful work or joy. I lacked the self-awareness necessary to obtain the best career path even though I had taught others the importance of obtaining that awareness.

I disengaged from my career path. My work had become a burden. Each day I would get up, lacking excitement to go to work, and would go through the motions to fulfill another meaningless day. I lacked purpose. I was stuck on the treadmill of disengagement. On a sticky Fourth of July day in Costa Rica, I was set free with a rejuvenating dream for my career and life.

My sister and I cracked open a fresh coconut after an exhilarating hike in the jungle. We listened to a familiar and appropriate tune for Independence Day: Grateful Dead's "Liberty." The song tells stories of people not living the way they were designed to live— and the emotional turmoil we feel when we are not aligned with our unique purpose. As I listened to the song, a mixture of salty tears and sweet coconut hit the corner of my lip. I realized I was not living a career aligned with my purpose. I was determined to find a new way. I was determined to find freedom from my burden.

I began to ask myself how I got there, retracing the steps that led me to my treadmill. How had my good intentions led me to into a meaningless career path? What in my past led me to chasing a mirage of success? As I questioned, the new answers were loud in my mind. My ambition to achieve a standard of success held up by an upwardly mobile society was leading me down a road where I felt unfulfilled in my life's purpose. I needed a new direction aligned with my unique passions and skills. I knew defining and finding that direction would lead to a more purpose-filled career. The burden in my heart lifted at the thought of a renewed perspective on success.

While I was unsure about the process, I resolved to pursue a career and a life of more happiness. I grabbed my journal and started to map out where I had been, where I was, and where I wanted to be. That first journal entry detailed the irony of how my pursuit of happiness had led me to be lost, feeling burdened, and toiling with meaningless work. Nonetheless, its tone was hopeful.

I could not ignore my experiences with those seeking a better career. When I experienced the treadmill of disengagement myself, I gained insight and empathy for others laboring under this burden. I was eager to design a process I could work through to gain greater awareness and obtain the career and life of my dreams.

My new pursuit of happiness was to help others in their pursuits—but with more lasting effect than I'd had before. By developing a simple process, I could help those who were unhappy, disengaged, or unemployed unlock career and life purpose. I left Costa Rica and arrived back home ready to jump off my treadmill and start a new business that would fulfill my purpose of helping others.

I love America and the dreams upon which our country is founded: life, liberty, and the pursuit of happiness. The beauty of the American Dream is that it encourages a process of personal empowerment; it was designed to free you to pursue your happiness and the best life you can live. Too often, however, job seekers chase after careers they believe will give them society's ideal of the American dream. This can lead job seekers to a pursuit of disengagement instead of happiness.

Over the next several chapters, we will help you shed some preconceptions about work, success, and the American Dream so you can discover your unique path, your Purpose Dreams.

Your Purpose Dreams

You were built to obtain your dreams. Dreams do more than merely give you something to shoot for; dreams provide a vision of where you will be. So often in this world, we think of dreams as unattainable. That is a lie: You have the ability to reach those dreams and live through their promise to your best life ever. As you clearly identify your dreams and work toward obtaining them, they will define and light your pathway.

There is no more critical venture in your life than to discover and work toward living your purpose. Your diligence in identifying your purpose will accelerate your pursuit of joy in your life. Your dreams will help you define that purpose.

The combination of your purpose and your dreams is a powerful mechanism to liberate you from the treadmill of disengagement. In the Renewal Journey ahead you will be equipped with the tools necessary to discover your purpose and your dreams, in short, your Purpose Dreams.

Do not define your Purpose Dreams by the standards of our culture. The standards of our culture may lead you to someone else's definition of life, liberty, and happiness. You were not created for someone else's dreams. The crux of the Renewal Journey is to translate your unique experiences into your Purpose Dreams. Your purpose dreams will catapult you to a loftier pursuit in life—one of purpose, freedom, and joy.

The A-to-Z of Obtaining Your Purpose Dreams

The predominant desire of the typical career seeker is to get a job quick and continue chasing society's idea of success. The job-seeking wisdom they gather covers topics such as how to build a resume, interview well, leverage their network, and obtain the next position based on their work history and experience. These are all important aspects of an effective career-seeking process; yet, without the self-awareness of an individual purpose, they will still end up on the treadmill of disengagement.

Let's view the career-seeking process through the alphabet, A to Z. The advice most seekers want (resume tips, interview best practices, networking, and so on) and most career counselors give is N-to-Z. The foundational element missing in most job-seeking processes comes earlier in the alphabet: A-to-M. This is where we discover true and unique stability, prosperity, and happiness within our working careers. The A-to-M pursuit requires contemplation, reflection, and tough questions. This part of the process aligns the seeker with greater self-awareness at the intersection of the past, present, and future. It requires discipline, faith, and courage, which might be why it is often skipped over to meet more immediate, but short-lived, satisfaction.

> *What then is the A-to-M? It is the journey that we are about to encounter together. It is an empowerment process to find a career path based on your dreams, and your dreams only. If taken seriously, the time-tested process that lies ahead will give you clarity to pursue your Purpose Dreams. Your Purpose Dreams are the foundation of a greater pursuit!*

The Renewal Journey

We have fine-tuned a process to help the unhappy, disengaged, or unemployed find more abundant life. This process has two cornerstones that make it unique: simplicity and effectiveness. There is nothing earth-shattering about it. Everyone can do it, but the process requires a commitment to contemplating one's true self and a desire for positive life change. We call this process the Renewal Journey.

The Renewal Journey asks you to spend forty-five minutes or an hour each day for ten days in order to gain awareness of your purpose and map out a plan to obtain it through your career search. In the pages ahead, you will be guided through this retreat. A career of richer purpose and joy will result from this investment in the Renewal Journey. This is the Purpose Promise.

You are the driving force behind the search for the career of your dreams. As you pursue this quest, you will experience new levels of engagement in all areas of your life. I was able to break free from the constraints that held me back from my ideal career purpose. You can too!

I lacked meaning in my work and life. I found purpose when I discovered who I was made to be.

I was burdened by my work. I found freedom when I mapped out my definition of true success.

I was lost, without the awareness and process to find a career of purpose. I found a life of joy when I retreated and renewed the vision for my life.

You will too!

As you read on, please ask yourself this question: *Do you sense there is a greater purpose designed for your life and work?*

Good news! You were designed *on* purpose *for* a purpose. In the pages ahead, you will be guided through a practical journey to gain purpose, freedom, and a life of joy!

As I embarked on the rainforest retreat in 2006, I had to let down my guard and admit that I was scared at times, exhilarated at others, and unable to do it alone. I had to trust those around me. I needed commitment and resilience to make it through the rainforest. You will need that same spirit of resilience to brave this journey. You are not alone. We are here to guide you, providing safe boundaries and assuring arrival at your destination.

I also had to equip myself before the journey. Kristin and Joshua helped me understand what I needed to bring. Among other necessities, my backpack contained a machete, an up-to-date map, a compass, knee-high boots, food for the journey, cooking gear, element-repelling clothing and of course my journal. The Renewal

Journey will require a similar combination. Along with trusting your guide and your spirit of resilience, you will also need some tools: a metaphorical machete to cut back lies of the past, a map to chart your course, and a compass to keep you pointed in the right direction.

On your Renewal Journey, each forty-five-minute retreat day will take you on a great adventure, revealing truths that will lead you to a new, exciting destination of self-awareness and purpose.

I thank you in advance for the opportunity to walk with you on this adventure. It requires vulnerability, courage, trust, and character. I will make you this promise:

If you trust this simple and effective process and pour your efforts into the details, the clarity that will come will not only point you to purposeful employment, but also a sustained level of immeasurable joy that will radically change your life.

Part Two: Preparing for Your Renewal Journey

chapter THREE

Finding Yourself and Being Yourself

"FEARLESSLY BE YOURSELF," I EXPLAINED to my nine-year-old daughter Bella, while walking her through a complicated issue she was having with some girls at school. This was a time in her life, fourth grade, when she was starting to find her identity and how that fits in with specific friend groups and expectations. It was an interesting parenting season for my wife and me as we watched our oldest child struggle to understand her unique makeup and how she fits in with the rest of the world. My wife and I recognized that we were on pivotal ground for developing her self-worth and her path in life.

The issue our daughter faced was the same one that we all face. The pressure to let the world dictate who she was to become was the same pressure that affects us all. Our daughter wanted to be accepted, successful, and stable. These desires are motivating variables for all of us. Ignoring the presence of these motivators can increase dissatisfaction at work, at home, and in relationships. Embracing their existence will unlock the potential to create the life we may see only in our dreams.

As we concluded our tearful conversation, Bella knew we would always be there to help her find her unique place in this world, a place that should not be defined by anybody but her. You, too, are uniquely made. Letting the realities of this world determine your dreams is selling yourself short of a life full of purpose, a purpose that is as unique as you are. To fearlessly be yourself, you will need to focus on knowing yourself!

Let's Focus on Knowing You

What do you want to be when you grow up?

Think back to your childhood. Do you remember how you answered this question?

Having three young kids, I get to watch as they creatively navigate through the dreams and possibilities of what they want to do. The question itself is a bit misleading, and maybe even telling, about the way we view work. What you do, vocationally, should not be the sole factor of who you are as a person; however, our culture puts considerable emphasis on the work you do to define your worth. That narrow perspective can keep you from uncovering your true purpose in life. This false ideology of limiting oneself based on societal standards is ingrained in us at a young age. Defining who you want to be, independent of those standards, is critical to establishing your Purpose Dreams.

What if we took a different perspective? What if we were asked at a young age, "How are you uniquely made?" We could then dream more effectively and ask, "How can you take the unique person that is you and use your talents and passions to best serve the world?" I know that might seem a bit idealistic, but if you are using your naturally ingrained talent and passions, you are more likely to be in the sweet spot of your career. When you are in the sweet spot of your career, you are more likely to be engaged. When you are engaged in work, you are more likely to be happy in life.

This all seems obvious, right? Then why is it that we rarely invest time in knowing ourselves?

Over the next few chapters, you will gain the opportunity to prepare yourself by reflecting on your unique makeup in three different areas that make up YOU: Yesterday, Ownership, and Understanding. Analyzing these foundational areas will help prepare for a successful Renewal Journey, the destination of which is obtaining your Purpose Dreams.

Yesterday

"Be here now." "Be present." "Live in the moment." "This moment is the only thing you have."

I can hear all these refreshing mottos as I finish up my invigorating yoga class. Don't get me wrong, I'm a big fan of yoga and being aware of the present moment, but is it possible that we have put so much emphasis on the current moment that we have lost the importance of the past and the future? All three work to create who we are. There is great wisdom in not dwelling on the past, but ignoring it altogether leads to a deceptive view of oneself. We need to take some time to accurately analyze those things in the past that make us who we are today.

As you go through your journey, we will help you look at the influences of your past, your Yesterday. These influences are foundational to the truth of who you are and will help define the Purpose Dreams that lie ahead.

Ownership

We are all more effective in life when we are proactive, not reactive. Too often, though, we see the world around us and what others are doing as the basis for how we do or don't want to live our lives. We react to the outer world instead of acting according to our own inner desires. Many aspects of our culture contribute to this tendency, for example, the obsession with social media and reality TV. But external expectations come from many other sources as well. During this Renewal Journey, you need to set aside those pressures to live someone else's ideals.

To combat a false self-identity, you need to have an intentional desire to focus on your own experiences and purpose in life. Looking to the external world to define your worth will eventually leave you feeling empty and abandoned. Ownership of your past, who you are, and who you want to be is an investment with significant returns.

As we go through our journey together, we will look at the factors to help you own who you are. As you gain this self-awareness, your Purpose Dreams will become more apparent and more obtainable.

Understanding

Maybe you remember Magic Eye puzzles: What appeared to be a random arrangement of tiny dots in many different colors hid a 3-D picture that only appeared to those who were able to divert their eyes. It took practice and persistence to calibrate your eyes and zone in on the hidden figure.

The way that we look at life through our different lenses will determine how we dream about ourselves. Thus, how you understand yourself will be critical to defining your Purpose Dreams. As we journey into understanding your perspective on success, we will uncover mindsets to banish. This transformation of mind is essential in gaining the right understanding.

You will need to spend some quality time embracing the full picture of your life: recalling your Yesterday, owning your experiences, and understanding right perspective. When you do so, a deeper personal revelation will pop out. There is more to you than meets the eye.

Your Renewal Journey Preparation

During my journey through the Costa Rican jungle, we had a clear destination in mind: clearing some land and creating a path to the retreat center we would build. The target was our purpose for being there, yet it was the journey toward that destination that provided the challenge. Being prepared with the right tools and awareness was vital to a safe journey.

This will also be the case in your Renewal Journey. You may have bought this book to find a more rewarding career path. You will reach that destination, but the journey that lies ahead will be the real prize. The next few chapters will prepare you for a safe and effective Renewal Journey.

One of our most valuable tools in Costa Rica was a machete. You, too, will need a metaphorical machete to cut through the lies that may have left you with a false concept of success. It will help you clear the path ahead as you cut back the brush that keeps you from your destination.

The most significant personal tool I had on my retreat in the jungle was my journal. Recording the deep thoughts and rich introspection that took place during that journey helped me to understand their significance. I took at least thirty minutes a day during those ten days to reflect on my experiences. I still have that journal, and reading through it holds me accountable to my Purpose Dreams.

As you prepare for your Renewal Journey, your journal is the tool where you will record what you are learning about yourself. This journal will hold the bits of wisdom that will eventually help you to define your Purpose Dreams. Preparing your mind with the right perspective on YOU is essential in making your Renewal Journey as full and rich as it can be.

Your journal can be as simple or elaborate as you choose. You can use paper and pen, or you might be more comfortable with a digital version. If you already have a journal, you might want to designate one section of it for this journey so that you can easily refer back to it in the future.

To maximize the impact of the Renewal Journey, we have developed *The Purpose Promise Workbook* that will give you a place to write your thoughts with handy prompts for the Renewal Journey. You can find that and other tools for your journey at www.purposepromise.org/tools

As you dive into the next few chapters of analyzing YOU, you will gain new awareness that is critical to preparing for your Renewal Journey. So, grab your machete and your journal as we cut back your past and clear a trail toward your Purpose Dreams.

chapter FOUR

Cutting through the Past: Yesterday

"Life can only be understood backwards; but it must be lived forwards." —Søren Kierkegaard

I HAVE FOND MEMORIES OF MY Grandma Marge and her captivating stories about her childhood during the Great Depression, family life on the farm, being swept off her feet by my grandfather after the war, and coaching my father in isolation as he battled for his life through polio. She had lived through a lot and obtained great wisdom. Her life, and how she lived it, has made a substantial impact on me and so many others.

She was an accomplished artist, and one of her talents was creating intricate quilts for special occasions and the special people in her life. When we visited her house, often she would be sitting at the table quilting away, surrounded by a sense of peace. When I was a young man, she gifted me one of these quilts. Nine boxes made up one colorful quilt, and each box represented a part of who I was: a baseball glove; a cat resembling our family pet, Marbles; a bowl of ice cream; a family picture of me, sis, Mom and Dad; the cover of *Where the Sidewalk Ends* (my favorite book at the time); a picture of Cincinnati (my hometown); my school's eagle mascot; an airplane to show my love for travel; and a big smile, to represent zeal for life.

At 101, she had lived life to the fullest with her community, her kids, her grandkids, and her great-grandkids. What a legacy! While she lay dying, many people came to her nursing home room to pay their last respects. She had been a significant person to them in some way. We were sad to lose her, but we celebrated her long, full life.

As our family came together upon her death to celebrate her life, we brought out dozens of quilts that she had given through the years. The quilts revealed aspects that made each person's life journey unique. These quilts showed how well Grandma understood and appreciated her loved ones—what they experienced and how that shaped their unique path. And suddenly I could see how each of the individual pieces of one quilt blended into a whole that was greater than the sum of its parts.

Grandma modeled how to live fully through the journey of life. Her passion for doing so impressed upon others. The insights I gained in reflecting on her life gave me a significant gift: genuine appreciation of my past.

Most of us don't take time to delve into our past to understand and appreciate the realities of our heritage, experiences, and uniqueness. We were designed to appreciate the compilation of experiences along life's journey.

Becoming aware of and appreciating your past will bring great insight into the process of developing your Purpose Dreams. As I look back at my past, I often analyze two variables to make sure the Purpose Dreams I define are consistent with who I want to be: the influence of the people in my past and the influence of the experiences of my past. To fully understand your past, your Yesterday, and embrace who you want to be, let's look at these two areas.

Analyzing the People in Your Yesterday

Pete was considering a career transition and had made a networking appointment with me. He came into my office well-dressed and with an agenda. He planned to tell me about his professional qualifications, explain his target companies to interview with, and describe how he would add value to them. He was well prepared and brimmed with confidence.

I listened respectfully as he made his way through his agenda. When he finished, I softly thanked him and asked if I could ask some clarifying questions.

"Of course," he said confidently.

I could sense Pete was chasing after career ambitions that were not uniquely his.

"Pete, how do you think your father's viewpoint of success has impacted your view of success?"

I have found this is one fundamental question to get to the heart of a matter that most "successful" men overlooked. The mixture of awkward silence and cumbersome nonverbal communication was one I had grown to expect. It never made me doubt the power of what would come next.

As Pete and I made our way through a conversation about his dad, how his dad viewed success, and how that impacted his view of success, I could feel the progressive energy build toward a more truth-laden conversation. Pete's journey toward a new career would take a turn toward a more important destination.

"Well, that was not what I expected, but it was awesome," said Pete as we left my office.

Over the past decade, I have walked with hundreds of career seekers just like Pete. Pete lacked important awareness about his past. He had never analyzed his most significant relationships or the critical moments of his life that influenced who he was striving to be. Delving into these memories can be tough, yet the outcome is always perspective changing.

It is time for a disclaimer. I'm not a shrink, nor do I enjoy when people are uncomfortable, yet time and time again I have watched great people chasing bad dreams based on the same type of mirage success that Pete sought. You and Pete are too important to live lives based on someone else's dreams. To find your Purpose Dream, you must become aware of who you are based on where you came from and what you have been through. You must have a clear understanding of Yesterday before you delve into a brighter Tomorrow.

I'll never forget the healing that took place on my journey in Costa Rica. At that time, I had been chasing after career dreams that were planted in me long ago. Some of these were consistent with who I wanted to be, yet others were based on the dreams of those people who had influenced my view of success. It was the same for Pete. Much of his journey had revolved around living up to his father's standards of success. Once he arrived at that destination, he continued trying to exceed those expectations. He was unhappy on his treadmill of disengagement. Once Pete started to redefine his success, I saw him come alive. Today, Pete is fulfilling his Purpose Dreams and is no longer burdened by work or the expectations planted in his Yesterday.

Identifying the people in your past who influenced your view of success is a valuable exercise to make sure your Yesterday is in proper perspective.

You have had many influencers. Take up your machete and cut through other people's expectations to your own view of success. Renew your success factors based on who *you* want to be!

Analyzing the Experiences in Your Yesterday

On the second morning of my life-changing retreat in Costa Rica, I awoke early to watch the sunrise. This would be the day for me to look back and understand my Yesterday and renew my Purpose Dreams. It was a dramatic and freeing day. As I grabbed my machete and headed toward the coconut tree, I wondered: How had my past experiences influenced the false precepts of my purpose in life?

After shaking a couple coconuts off of the tree and breaking one open, I ran to my backpack to grab my journal. Revealing thoughts were flowing as quickly as the refreshing water from the coconut. I wrote at the top of the page: MY IDENTITY IS NOT IN MY ACCOMPLISHMENTS

I am a goal setter. I crave structure, lists, and deadlines. I have learned to value these things because they get me to accomplishments. But continuously striving for ever greater achievements is exhausting! I realized that I was dealing with an idol in my life that was keeping me from my true purpose. This idol was Performance.

I try to keep my performance idol in check, but it tends to control me when I make my performance the object of adoration. I learned from those around me to equate self-worth with accomplishment. Past experiences of perceived success made me feel worthy in the eyes of others. Somewhere along the way, I started feeling most valuable when I was successful. Accomplishments that became the objects of my desire included winning the game, making more money, getting the promotion, acing the test, or graduating with a new degree. None of these are inherently bad, but when they became the crux of my identity, I lost the proper perspective on my life's priorities. Accomplishments are good; I'm not downplaying that. Yet, as I look back at my experiences, the continual striving for accomplishments reinforced efforts to reach destinations that were not consistent with my best life.

Revelation struck as I journaled that morning in the Costa Rican rainforest. Compulsively prioritizing accomplishments had driven my view of success. The shame I felt at the realization turned to hope as I vowed not to let my view of a successful life be based solely on the false constructs from my performance idol.

Whenever I catch myself striving for accomplishment, I stop and ask myself if effort toward that accomplishment is consistent with my Purpose Dreams. This crucial question has kept me from a lot of wrong paths and focused the path toward my fullest life, abundant with purpose, freedom, and joy.

The performance idol is common among career seekers. If they aren't aware of its presence, it can lead to some misaligned priorities. Maybe you don't wrestle with this particular idol. But, know that analyzing your past experiences will help you find the idols keeping you away from your path to your purpose. The factors that program success in our minds are hidden and even subconscious.

Your future is bright, but I urge you not to let the people, nor the experiences of your Yesterday, create success factors that dim that future. As you journey into Yesterday, identify your aspirations. Cut through them to ensure they are based on who you want to be, not just a false sense of self-worth associated with Yesterday's influences.

You are a masterpiece created for a unique purpose. As you begin to cut through your Yesterday, let the new awareness of your past influences renew your Purpose Dreams.

Grab Your Journal

« If you had a quilt made for you, what would your nine individual boxes be? How do those boxes represent the experiences or influences that make you unique?

chapter FIVE

Cutting Through the Past: Ownership

"Everything can be taken from a man but one thing: the last of human freedoms—to choose one's attitude in any given set of circumstances, to choose one's own way."

—Viktor E. Frankl, *Man's Search for Meaning*

WHEN MY WIFE AND I GOT MARRIED, we eagerly purchased a house in a hip part of town. We passionately pursued our new neighborhood and the effort to make it the best it could be. We both jumped in and got our hands dirty to be a part of the change we wanted to see. The community had a passionate core of volunteers and professional leaders, but after a couple years of progress, we seemed to plateau as a community.

This plateau boggled us. We expected the progress to multiply excitement, but that did not happen. We brainstormed tactics and took inventory of the core leaders. We finally identified our issue. Sustainable progress would only be organized if we could get more folks excited about regular involvement. But statistics showed us that only 40 percent of the people in our community had some stake in improving it.

After a few months of digging into that question, we discovered a stat that had apparent correlation. The percentage of home ownership in our community was only 45 percent. Our tactics changed. We wanted our neighborhood to be seen as a great place to buy a home. In the years following the shift in strategy, we saw a 15 percent increase in ownership, and we were able to attract more active volunteers. This more extensive base of volunteers made sustainable improvements, and the community is now touted as one of our city's best places to live.

So, what in the world does this have to do with the journey to greater purpose, freedom, and the pursuit of joy? It's all about ownership. There is a significant psychological difference between renting something and owning it. The same can be said about the perspective we take in life. Initiating action to make a better life is more likely to take place if you are in the driver's seat of progress. Ownership of your past experiences, your emotions, and your decisions are the essential ingredients to embracing change and finding your purpose.

When we habitually blame others or point fingers, we tend to have a skewed view of reality, which, in turn, can hinder us from seeing the best path for our lives. Taking the machete to any areas of your life that you have not owned will change the way you look at your past and dream about your future.

Let's begin the journey to ownership with a few questions.

Grab Your Journal

- « Do you blame others for the disengagement you feel at work or home?
- « Do you own areas of your life that are less than optimal, or do those areas own you?
- « Are you or were you a victim of a particular circumstance?

I have learned, mostly through my failures, that when I expect life to adapt to me, I usually end up disappointed. Conversely, when I mindfully adapt to what life throws at me, then I can be at peace in almost any circumstance. I don't do this perfectly, but I am getting better at recognizing when I'm falling into blaming and self-pity. Owning my life and my circumstances has helped me envision greater Purpose Dreams. No matter how hard it has been, today is the day to begin to own your past and renew your journey.

Own your Hardships

Along your Renewal Journey, it is vital for you to realize that memories can haunt your ability to identify your Purpose Dreams. One of the best ways to overcome past hardships is to begin to take ownership of healing painful events and memories in your past. We need to be careful not to allow those painful experiences to own us. It can be difficult to do this on your own, so don't be afraid or embarrassed to seek help. A strong support system, and even working with a licensed professional, can be invaluable here, especially if you've suffered significant trauma in your past.

Emotions are often subconscious drivers of our actions and reactions. Some of those hidden emotions were driving my behaviors, and I was clueless about their power until I owned their existence. The Renewal Journey will help you begin to uncover these powerful forces that might be limiting your quest for your true purpose.

> **Grab Your Journal**
>
> « How about you? Are you…
> « Holding grudges?
> « Feeling shame?
> « Frustrated with the world around you?
> « Feeling empty?

A good portion of the Renewal Journey will help you rewrite the redemption story of your hardships. You will break the pattern of your hardships owning you, and a new-found freedom will propel the discovery of your Purpose Dreams.

Own Your Purpose

Victor Frankl's memoir, *Man's Search for Meaning,* documents his psychological explorations while a prisoner in the Auschwitz concentration camp during World War II. One of his many conclusions that stood out for me was that when a person owns a purpose in life, he or she will push through hardships with greater resilience. Frankl further concludes that the inability to find meaning can make the anxieties of life overwhelming and lead to a lack of happiness.

This was and remains convicting to me. We all face adversities, but ownership of your purpose differentiates the free from the burdened. A lack of purpose is one of the main things powering the treadmill of disengagement. Don't be one of those statistics. Your success depends on you owning your unique purpose. Once you have journeyed to find it, nobody can take it away from you. Once you own your Purpose Dreams, you will unlock the chains that keep you from abundant purpose, freedom, and joy.

> **Grab Your Journal**
>
> « How could owning your hardships free you?
> « How could owning your purpose help you navigate life's
>   ups and downs?

Owning your hardships and your purpose takes effort. There are probably some giants lingering in your yesterday that you will need to wrestle with before ownership is embraced. The Renewal Journey will walk you through healing your past, forgiving those that you may have a grudge against, and freeing you from mistakes you have made. As we move into the Renewal Journey, begin to use your machete to cut back what you can to clear the path to greater ownership!

chapter SIX

Cutting Through the Past: Understanding

"Above all, don't lie to yourself. The man who lies to himself and listens to his own lie comes to a point that he cannot distinguish the truth within him, or around him, and so loses all respect for himself and for others."

—Fyodor Dostoyevsky, *The Brothers Karamazov*

ONCE YOU RECOGNIZE THE TRUTH IN your Yesterday and Own your experiences, you will be in a better position to Understand the right perspective on past and present realities. A faulty understanding often stems from a mindset of "what if." When we seek a reality that is not our own, we tend to lose our proper perspective.

Along the Renewal Journey, you will identify many "what ifs" that are keeping you from your best self. The Journey will help you develop processes to focus on "what is," not "what if." Distinguishing between the two will set you toward your Purpose Dreams.

In my life, I have noticed that my "what if" mentality can lead to three emotions that keep me from my understanding myself: envy, shame, and fear. I call these my "what if" emotions. I am hopeful that sharing how these "what if" emotions have impacted my journey will help you begin to recognize your "what if" emotions.

Understanding Envy: What if I had _____ (fill in the blank)?

My wife has straight hair; her best friend has naturally curly hair. One day the two were getting ready to go out for the evening. I barely have any hair, so it is hard to understand why it takes them so long to get ready. But I was amazed when I realized that my wife was curling her straight hair, and her best friend was straightening her curly hair. I guess it is human nature to want what we don't have.

Have you ever caught yourself thinking: "I would be so much happier if..."

On my days when real fulfillment seems to be lacking, I have caught myself thinking envy-driven wishes. Imagining a better reality based on someone else's journey distracts me from understanding my own past and present realities.

Grab Your Journal

« What is it you desire that you believe would bring you more happiness?

Nobody but you should determine your success factors. The Renewal Journey will free you from the "what ifs" associated with envy. Envy often breeds comparison that will keep you from your unique Purpose Dreams. Understand this: You are a masterpiece. You don't need what others have to live a joy-filled life.

Understanding Shame: What if I had not done _____(fill in the blank)?

Shame has a considerable impact on our health, our happiness, and our purpose. I was reminded of this recently as I walked with a good friend through one of his greatest challenges. Paul's son was battling depression, addicted to drugs, and becoming more isolated each day. Paul confided in me at a local coffee shop. He was a broken man, lacking direction and hope. We made our way through all the facts of his son's current state to get to Paul's feelings about it. He broke down as he admitted to wondering what he could have done as a father to prevent this. I listened and cried with him; then he looked to me with eyes that said, "What should I do?"

Before he could plan, he had to remember how great a dad he was. As we recalled memories of his parenting, the right perspective started to take form. He recalled the many times he had helped his other kids through difficult circumstances. Then, as better understanding prevailed, his increased confidence to handle "what is" erased the shame of "what if."

The "what ifs" were imprisoning him. How could he deal with this tough scenario with his son if he, himself, was not seeing the right perspective? He eventually admitted that his fathering was not the cause of his son's situation. This understanding helped us to phase two, the plan for how to help his son in the "what is."

I am pleased to report that Paul's son is healed from his battle with mental illness and addiction. He is now a thriving young man. Paul and I continue to hold each other accountable not to let the "what ifs" in our life keep us from navigating the "what is."

Too often we fall prey to questioning our past and present decisions, actions, and circumstances. Life happens, and you are not to blame for everything going on around you. Re-engage the "what ifs" and categorize them with better understanding so you can deal more effectively with "what is."

We will take a deep dive into this process as we make our way on this Renewal Journey, but for now, start to recognize the pattern of blaming yourself. Begin to take control of the shame-filled "what ifs." You must first be aware of their presence to work through them.

Grab Your Journal

« Are you blaming yourself for any current circumstances?

The lies of shame can keep you from your Purpose Dreams. Understand this: You are not a mistake. Nobody is perfect. Learn from your mistakes. Don't let your mistakes create your identity.

Understanding Fear: What if _____ (fill in the blank) happens?
Fear was a big part of our reality when we had our third child, Lydia. When Lydia was born, she was perfect in our sight. The day we all had waited for had arrived, and the child we imagined was in our arms. The first ten minutes of her life outside the womb were magical. It was the eleventh minute that started the chaos every parent fears. The doctor took her from my arms as my wife was resting from her C-Section. The doctor explained that they needed to perform some testing right away. The reasoning was abstract, but they revealed there were some concerns with what appeared to be a rash on her skin and a possible blood disease. Watching my thirty-minute-old princess get blood drawn, crying uncontrollably, and not being able to comfort her, was one of the most challenging moments in my life.

Once tests were underway and our baby girl was back in our arms, the flood of emotions rolled over us. We were joy-filled to have her, but the fear and anxieties of what could come next were paralyzing our state of bliss. We met with multiple doctors that morning as they explained the precautionary nature of these tests and the probabilities of what the tests could reveal. As we awaited outcomes and addressed possibilities, the "what ifs" of our future overtook all thought.

Fear has power over our minds. When faced with fear of the future, irrational thoughts trump the right perspective. For me, my wife, and our family, we remained hopeful that Lydia would be perfectly healthy, but the more time that went on between doctor visits, the more fear trumped the joy we should have been experiencing. Thank God the "what ifs" we created were not our path with Lydia. Tests eventually ruled out what we feared it could be. After a few months, her rash completely disappeared, and she was a happy and healthy baby.

I am certainly not trying to dismiss the reality of planning how to navigate through the ever-changing ebbs and flows of our lives; however, when we let our minds go too far toward the "what ifs," we let those thoughts and emotions dictate our "what is." It is almost impossible not to fear the worst in crisis situations, but we can't let those fears crowd out all reason. Right perspective of "what is" can alleviate the power that hovers over the fear-filled "what ifs."

For now, begin to examine the "what ifs" that pop up when you imagine your future. Rather than let them drive your awareness, drive them toward a greater awareness of "what is."

Grab Your Journal

« Are there any "what ifs" that you fear are keeping you from enjoying the "what is"?

Fear will keep you from your Purpose Dreams. Fearing the future will not lead you to the life you were designed to live.

You Can Control your Mind

While it is a myth that we only use 10 percent of our our brain, it's true that how we use our brain leaves plenty of opportunity for improvement. Few of us effectively process the information we take in. When we commit to filter the way we react to gathered information, our minds live up to their untapped power. When we retreat to gain greater understanding, we unlock fantastic potential for our thought patterns and the norms that create our behaviors. Your life will only reach its potential if you spend the time and energy necessary to gain the right perspective by controlling your mind.

By cutting through your Yesterday, Owning your experiences, and Understanding right perspective, you will increase your ability to control your mind. This is the essential posture to take into your Renewal Journey. It is time to retreat to renew. You are now well prepared. Let the Journey begin!

chapter SEVEN

Your Renewal Journey Guide

IT WOULD HAVE BEEN IMPOSSIBLE TO navigate through life in the Costa Rican rainforest without a good plan. If it were not for my guides, Kristin and Joshua, and how they prepared me for my journey, I would have been a dead man...literally. There is no way I would have known how to steer clear of venomous scorpions. I would not have known how to keep the ants (whose feet contained trace elements of hydrochloric acid) off my skin. I would not have been able to recognize the poisonous berries that looked so much like fruit I brought home from the supermarket. My guides gave me the boundaries I needed to make my journey safe, structured, and effective.

There are dangerous factors present for you on your Renewal Journey, too. Lingering subconscious factors such as self-deceit, family influence, wrong perspective, and a mirage of success will attempt to keep you on your treadmill of disengagement. This Renewal Journey contains the boundaries to keep these unwanted patterns back and ensure that you stay on a straight and safe path toward your Purpose Dreams!

The Renewal Journey is a ten-day commitment, forty-five minutes a day. If you want your life to change you have to change your life. The 450-minute Renewal Journey has changed many lives, and it will change your life, too. The return on investing the time is exponential.

If you embrace a higher level of self-awareness through this retreat, you will define your Purpose Dreams. These Purpose Dreams will set the course for you to obtain a more purpose-filled career path. That is the destination of your Renewal Journey; however, the journey to get there will lead you to an even greater reward: sustainable and life-changing purpose, freedom, and joy.

Your Purpose Guide

As your partner in this journey, this book will be an excellent guide; however, you might like a more personal approach to this retreat journey. If that is the case, we are here for you. We have developed a Purpose Promise organization that will connect you to a Purpose Guide. The combination of your personal retreat time and a time of reflection with your Purpose Guide is the most effective way to engage this retreat.

Your Purpose Guide is a highly trained and proven coach, familiar with the path you are on toward renewal. Your Purpose Guide is a resource for you on this journey. We genuinely want to journey with you. If you can, please take advantage of this offering by visiting us at www.purposepromise.org.

You will be able to handpick your Purpose Guide and set up your first meeting via video, phone or email. Visit www.purpose-promise.org/tools to maximize your Renewal Journey. We are excited to walk with you as your proven guide!

Your Retreat Plan: Eliminate Distraction

About two months ago I called all my closest friends and family to let them know I would not be reachable on Sundays anymore. I wanted to make sure they were aware so they did not think something terrible had happened to me when they could not reach me on Sundays. I decided to make Sundays a phone-free day. My smartphone was captivating way too much of my attention. I noticed myself staring at it and missing the great things happening around me.

I vulnerably admit that I have not been able to do it. I have not had one Sunday since I made this commitment that I was able to eliminate my phone's presence 100 percent. I have put reasonable restrictions on its use, but I'm amazed at how much I feel I might miss if my loved ones can't reach me. I do not get email or look at any apps, but still feel I need to have access to the phone. This says a lot about how much distraction creeps into my daily process. I'm getting better, I promise, but still struggle to not be a slave to the smartphone.

What distracts you from your daily rhythms?

Each of us has our distractions, and eliminating them is the first step in healthy retreating. When I am retreating, it is the one time I never bring my phone. I make sure I get away. Life is full of demands and people who want attention. For me to be fully present in my retreat time, I need to get away from these distractions and demands.

The second step in healthy retreating is planning it. If you are married and have kids, this must be done with your spouse to ensure agreement. If loved ones rely on you in any way, please do communicate with them the intent of your retreat time. Put up boundaries and infrastructure to make sure you can be focused. Undistracted focus is imperative to your Renewal Journey.

It is highly unlikely that you will have ten full days to dedicate to your retreat journey. That is not a problem. At the very least, please set aside forty-five minutes of personal retreat time for ten consecutive days. This commitment will radically change your life and help you establish your Purpose Dreams.

The third step is to consider utilizing your Purpose Guide. If you are willing and able to use the Guide, we will schedule a debrief with you after certain days of your retreat. Sharing your journey with a Purpose Guide will maximize its reward. The more time you can invest in the Renewal Journey, the more you will get out of it.

So, let's map out your plan.

Grab Your Journal

STEP 1: *Eliminate Distractions*
What distractions might you need to eliminate to be entirely focused when you are retreating?

« Make sure your phone is nowhere close, so you are not tempted to stare at it. Get to a place with no screens for your personal retreat time.

STEP 2: *Plan*
What date will you start your Renewal Journey retreat that you can continue for ten consecutive days?

« Make sure to schedule this time like you would an important meeting for the whole week you have chosen. Do not break the commitment you have made to retreat. This should be considered the top priority on your calendar.

What do you need to organize to ensure you can fulfill your time commitments for your retreat?

« What tasks may creep up that you could anticipate? How can you proactively eliminate, delegate, or automate these tasks?

Who do you need to communicate with to ensure you are not bothered or distracted during your retreat time?

« Make sure your family is aware and supportive of this plan. Make sure your work support is aware of this plan.

STEP 3: *Purpose Guide*

Are you willing to maximize your retreat by partnering with a proven guide?

« If so, visit www.purposepromise.org/tools, and we will take care of the details. Remember, this is a resource to ensure you reach the goals of your retreat. If not, that is OK. We will still be here for you if you decide you want a guide during the journey.

Thank you for taking this process seriously and mapping it out. Your commitment will make all the difference!

Part Three: Your Ten-Day Renewal Journey

Know Yourself: Understanding and Owning Yesterday

WAY TO GO! HERE YOU ARE, READY TO dig in and find those Purpose Dreams. Remember to reduce distraction and give at least forty-five minutes to this foundational day of your retreat.

Two poorly constructed psychological realities often drive the way we seek a career; in fact, they are detrimental toward finding a purposeful career path. They let the outside work world diminish your own unique journey. We need to call them out here at the beginning to ensure you can recognize and eliminate them if they creep in during this retreat.

1. You are not what you have done.

It is typical for career seekers to look at their past work experiences and pigeonhole themselves into what they have done. What you have done professionally is part of who you are, but there is so much more to the picture of you. Treadmills of disengagement are full of those who believe they are what they have done. If they move from one job to a similar one, they may may have a slightly different landscape or people around, but the treadmill is ultimately the same. This ideology rarely leads to a more fulfilling long-term career.

What you have done in your career is important in your career search; however, *you* are not solely what you have done. Knowing this is essential as we move forward into our analysis of your past work experience.

2. You are not what is out there.

Job seekers typically go out to the job boards, put in their keywords, and then apply if they meet 50 percent of the qualifications and 50 percent of the job description. This approach results in job seekers who apply to 40 or 50 jobs per day. This is not the targeted approach seasoned with self-awareness that is going to lead to obtaining your Purpose Dreams. Career seekers who take this approach are essentially concluding "what is out there is who I am." That could not be further from the truth. Who you are is entirely independent of what the work world offers on the job boards.

Any efficient and effective career-seeking process starts with the foundation of you, all of who you are. As you move through this ten-day journey, please be conscious of these faulty mindsets. What you need to craft your Purpose Dreams and obtain a career that fulfills them is wisdom!

The Language of Experience: Understanding and Owning Your Yesterday

Would you rather be knowledgeable or wise?

Seriously, consider that question. Knowledge and wisdom are different. What differentiates them? Experience. Wisdom is earned when we realize our experience is a teacher.

America's favorite pastime reminded me of this. I was coaching my five-year-old son's tee ball team. Coaching five-year-olds in anything is a challenge, especially baseball on a dirt field. I learned a lot about young boys that season. During a sixty-minute base-ball game, most of the kids would spend at least forty of those minutes playing in the dirt. We learned the basics though, like how to eat sunflower seeds and chant, "batter-batter-batter, swing batter!"

Out of the ten kids, one was ambitious to learn the game. Nolan showed great athletic ability and an insatiable desire to be the best on the team (not much of a claim on this team!). After we finished batting one-half inning of our first game, the lad came running up to me, "Coach, coach, coach," he yelled.

"What is it Nolan?" I asked, imagining he got stung by a bee.

"Can I please play shortstop this inning?"

"Absolutely, buddy."

"Great! So...where is it?"

I could only imagine that Nolan had caught wind of the excitement of playing shortstop, yet he had never experienced it, so he had no idea where it was. What a classic depiction of the difference between knowledge and wisdom!

So much of the rhetoric of our lives is based on the facts we pick up along the way. We live in the age of information. Being constantly bombarded by it makes us a knowledge-rich society, but mere knowledge is not power. Knowledge understood through experience is wisdom. Wisdom is power!

The language of experience leads to wisdom. Yep, you read that right: the language of experience. Our unique experiences in life are a communication medium. The gradual growth of under-standing who you are based on your experiences will change the way you look at the information that is constantly served to you. Smartphones, tablets, news outlets, and others' viewpoints must be filtered to discern the truth for yourself. The language of experience brings forth understanding to help you gain wisdom. Knowledge will not lead you to your Purpose Dreams; wisdom is the key to create them!

When we fail to own our Yesterday, our understanding distorts the reality of who we are. When we embrace the lies we have been told about ourselves, we rent someone else's thoughts. When we let the world define what success looks like for us, we subscribe to another's view of happiness. Doing so is why 75 percent of America's workforce is disengaged from their work.

Today, you will be plotting your life and career experiences. The language of your experience will bring forth the wisdom necessary to guide your Renewal Journey to the destination of your Purpose Dreams. As I made my way through the uncharted Costa Rican jungle, my up-to-date map contained the direction to reach my destination. On your Renewal Journey, your life and career graphs are your maps.

Life Graph Exercise

The crux of this retreat is to translate the language of your experience into your Purpose Dreams. Doing so is one of the simplest, yet most profound, exercises you will ever experience. I have walked hundreds of career seekers through this exercise. The participants have ranged from entry-level workers to C-level executives in a wide variety of industries. Without fail, the feedback to this simple exercise of graphing one's career and life is paradigm shifting.

Your Life Graph will look like this:

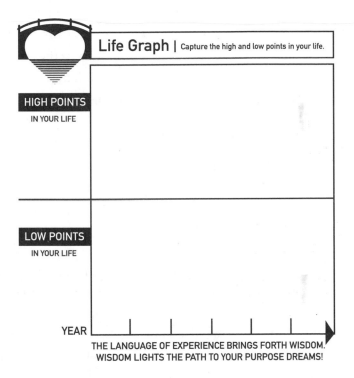

Life Graph | Capture the high and low points in your life.

HIGH POINTS
IN YOUR LIFE

LOW POINTS
IN YOUR LIFE

YEAR

THE LANGUAGE OF EXPERIENCE BRINGS FORTH WISDOM.
WISDOM LIGHTS THE PATH TO YOUR PURPOSE DREAMS!

Start with your earliest memories and chart your most poignant memories using a dot based on whether you would consider them high points in your life, low points in your life, or somewhere in between. Continue to do this throughout your whole past. Be as detailed as possible and think, think hard; think back to what was and let your yesterday unfold onto the paper.

We recommend you spend at least an hour on the life graph. This is the foundation of a healthy analysis of your past, so it should be given its due time.

Don't worry about the learning from these experiences yet; simply map them out on your life graph as they come to you.

Try to remember the age you were when these pivotal moments took place. Jot the ages down on the graph as they come.

There will be moments that are hard for you to relive. Give yourself the time you need to absorb the emotion of the moment. Remember that your Purpose Guide is only a click away, at www. purposepromise.org/tools, if you want a trained and empathetic ear during any of these moments.

Be aware of the feelings you may have about the people in your life who were part of the pivotal moments that you are now plotting. Don't let these feelings, positive or negative, be a hindrance. We will deal with these emotions soon. They are real and powerful and demand ample time and reflection.

The more time you can take to bring back memories and plot them on your life graph, the better. Your life is made up of many moments, some good and some not so good. Some memories that were deeply buried will start to arise during this exercise.

Don't worry about the look of your graph. This is for you and you only to gain the wisdom needed to develop your Purpose Dreams. You can also get an electronic form of your life graph at www.purposepromise.org.

Career Graph Exercise
Now we will seek wisdom through your experiences in your career.

Your Career Graph will look like this:

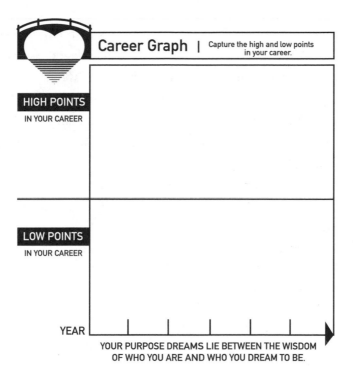

Career Graph | Capture the high and low points in your career.

HIGH POINTS
IN YOUR CAREER

LOW POINTS
IN YOUR CAREER

YEAR

YOUR PURPOSE DREAMS LIE BETWEEN THE WISDOM
OF WHO YOU ARE AND WHO YOU DREAM TO BE.

It might be a bit more difficult for you to recall jobs, seasons, or days that were pivotal along your career journey. If you are struggling, here are good questions to help you remember:

When (day, job, or season) were you fired up to get out of bed and get to work?

Plot these as high points on your career graph.

When (day, job, or season) were you hitting the snooze bar, dreading going to work?

Plot these as low points on your career graph.

Go through your career and get as much detail as you can. We will work through some questions that will bring greater insight into your career graph, but for now, relive those seasons and jobs and jot them high, low, and everywhere in between.

You have just designed the map to reach the destination of your Purpose Dreams. In the days to come, we will look at these pivotal moments through a microscope to reveal truths about you. Take a look at your life graph and your career graph. There is a lot of wisdom on the path you have plotted. The combination of the life graph and the career graph will bring forth the wisdom needed to craft your Purpose Dreams.

For now, let your mind freely process what you have gathered based on your graphs, and prepare yourself for the next, more intimate leg of the journey.

day TWO

Perspective on the Past:
Understanding Yesterday

IT DOES NOT MATTER HOW QUICKLY you get somewhere if it is the wrong place to go. We were reminded of that one frustrating late afternoon in the Costa Rican jungle. Lost in the rainforest was a new kind of lost. You don't want to be caught on the wrong side of the rainforest as night falls. We all agreed to stop and put our heads together around the map. We could see where we needed to head but didn't know in what direction we were headed. For most of my life a compass had been mainly a toy; but that day it was pivotal to our survival. Without the right direction, we would have continued to go down the wrong path.

You now have your up-to-date map: your career and life graphs. The vantage points and landmarks will only be helpful if analyzed the right way. Today's process of connecting the dots will be your compass on the Renewal Journey. After today you will be going in the right direction toward your Purpose Dreams.

Connecting the Dots

As you connect the dots on your career and life graphs, common denominators will present themselves. These common denominators will be great teachers. The questions that follow will help you analyze your life and career graphs. Not all the questions will apply to you, but go through each one seeking the wisdom you need to own your yesterday.

Be aware of your feelings, but don't let them drive you away from any of the questions. Go through your graphs looking for the evidence needed to answer these questions. Add more detail to your graphs, as these questions reveal memories you may not have plotted on Day One.

Be aware of any questions that trigger a spike in emotion for you. These are the ones that hold the keys to unlocking some burdens you are carrying. It will not be fun to work through these more difficult areas, but they are important, so don't skip over them. The depth of this journey is based on your honesty and the courage that comes from working through it.

Don't forget to connect with us at www.purposepromise.org, if you would like a Purpose Guide to help in the analysis of your past. Our guides are equipped to help. At some point, this journey will feel uncomfortable, but don't let that keep you from the purpose, freedom, and joy that lies ahead.

Perspective on Hardship

Yesterday's hardships, the lower points on your graphs, may be hard to revisit; however, they contain essential wisdom. Analyzing past hardships will reveal character patterns that have become habitual. The questions that follow will help you pinpoint whether you should become more intentional about staying away from some realities. This can take many forms, depending on your yesterday, but if you own your difficult yesterdays you will inevitably gain wisdom.

A friend told me that as he went through his life and career graph exercise, he realized that many of his so-called failures in life, the lower points on his graph, were the greatest character builders. He even concluded that one of the lowest parts on his life graph is now one of the top five best things that ever happened to him.

Adversity drives resilience. Resilience drives character. Character leads to greater hope, and greater hope changes you. As you work through the lower parts of your career and life graphs, seek and celebrate how you have grown through the adversity you have experienced. I'm not downplaying the pain you went through at the time. But that's only one side of the coin. Becoming aware of the growth that may have resulted gives you a new perspective. You can now see the whole picture. Be proud of how you fought through adversity. Celebrate and own your character!

Grab Your Journal

Questions to Explore on Your Life Graph

« What common denominators pop out about the low points on your life graph?

« What environments/factors should you steer clear of in your life based on perceived hardships?

« Was there a common geography based on the low points of your life graph?

« How has the adversity in your life grown your character?

Questions to Explore on Your Career Graph

« What common denominators pop out about the low points on your career graph?

« What environments/factors should you steer clear of in your career based on the low points of your career graph?

« Why did you have a propensity to hit the snooze button during the low points of your career graph?

« How has the adversity in your career grown your character?

Perspective on Success

What does success mean to you?

This is a core question for your Renewal Journey. As you define your Purpose Dreams you will learn that your happiness is not solely derived from career success as the world defines it. Many factors make up what success means to you.

Happiness is personal to each of us. The right perspective on your success and the higher points on your graphs will help you understand your own definition of success.

There is undoubtedly a correlation between career success and happiness; however, many of us have bought into the lie that career success will lead to material abundance, and material abundance will lead to happiness. Too often this leads to a feeling of emptiness once we gain the world's possessions but still don't feel happy.

There is nothing inherently wrong with money or material possessions. In fact, if viewed with right perspective, money can do great things in your life. But an unbalanced desire for money throws a wrench in its goodness.

Once an employee's monetary needs are met, the motivational value of money dramatically decreases; other intrinsic motivators (purpose-driven work, opportunity to grow skills, work/life balance, etc.) significantly increase. At the core of this psychological fact is the truth that obtaining money beyond our current financial needs is not going to buy us happiness.

On Day Six of this retreat, we will delve deep into provision. We will analyze the element of material provision relative to your relational, motivational, and spiritual needs. Through the analysis of your needs and wants, you will define your vision of success and your Purpose Dreams. For now, be wary of determining success solely on the money you make. As you answer the questions below, seek out the common denominators that made you feel a sense of purpose, freedom, and joy. These are the seasons when you were living your best life.

No longer must we believe what the world tells us success is. It is time to own your understanding of success. You are not a square peg in the round hole of the American Dream.

As you go through the questions below and come to greater self-awareness, realize that the success of your life was not accidental. Common denominators set you up for past success. Having the intention to understand these factors and reinforce them will lead to new Purpose Dreams.

Grab Your Journal

Questions to Explore on your Life Graph

« What do your high points in life reveal to you about things you should focus upon?

« What skills, passions, or talents were you using at the highest points of your life graph?

« What environments/factors should you reproduce in your life based on the high points of your life graph?

« Was there a common geography based on the low points of your life graph?

« How should you prioritize and be intentional about certain areas of your life?

Questions to Explore on your Career Graph

« What common denominators pop out about the high points on your career graph?

« What made you excited to get out of bed during the high points of your career?

« If you were working within a team, how was this team constructed that made it effective? Ineffective?

« What type of environment were you working in at the high points of your career?

« How much autonomy/direction were you given at the high points of your career?

« What skills, passions, or talents were you using at the high points of your career?

« What do the high points in your career reveal about things you should focus upon?

« How should you prioritize and be intentional about certain areas of your career?

Your past hardships and successes reveal so much about your journey. I'm hopeful you are starting to see some revelation around lies you have believed and truths that will set you free. You are headed in the right direction: toward your Purpose Dreams!

Forgiveness: Freedom from the Subconscious Threats Lingering from your Hardships

"*Terciopelo!*" This was one of the most alarming Spanish words that I learned during my journey to Costa Rica. The terciopelo is the most feared snake in the rainforest. The natives cautioned us about the unpredictable and deadly terciopelo more than any other danger throughout our journey. But I was determined that the threat of this predator was not going to keep me from my destination. With proper boots, I lessened the terciopelo's power over me. I was able to carry on, enjoying my journey with a keen eye to ensure my safety.

On your Renewal Journey an unexpected enemy could block your right perspective. Today, you will be looking back at your Yesterday hardships to identify and eliminate any lingering threats to your purpose and the freedom and joy that lie ahead.

You were hurt in the past, and you will be hurt again. This is a reality of the world we live in. If you remain unaware of the emotions associated with your hardships, you will fail to reach your destination. Their presence could be more dangerous than a venomous snake, but by re-engaging them in the safe space of your Renewal Journey, you will eliminate their power over you.

It is well-documented that past hardships can cause physical and mental illness if not dealt with in a healthy way. Today, we will work on eliminating the guilt, shame, and resentment that might be keeping you from owning and understanding your yesterday.

Understanding Hardships that Were Out of Your Control

As you look back at your life and career graphs, some memories make you ask, "Why?" These are often events that happened to you that were out of your control. They caused much pain and heartache. It could be a loss of a loved one, a natural disaster, an accident, or a hardship that doesn't seem fair. When the subconscious emotions associated with these memories are swept under the rug and not embraced, they cause further pain. If you process them effectively, you will discover a more profound perspective on life that can help you reach your Purpose Dreams.

Everyone, no matter his or her belief system, experiences the broken world we live in. Belief in a Higher Power is not going to save you from experiencing difficult and uncontrollable circumstances. Processing life's tough questions, however, can get you to the core of your beliefs about life, creation, and God. One of the primary reasons people tend not to have a relationship with their Maker is that they have a hard time believing an all-loving God could allow the pain and suffering we experience in this life. I understand this argument and have wrestled through it myself. The wrestling with it is where the healing and right perspective begins.

Most of us would not admit that we hold a grudge against God, but many of us do. Eliminating the pursuit of God due to past hardships has troubling consequences for the way we view the world. Cynicism becomes our default mode. Coming to right perspective with the brokenness of the world is the first step in healing much of the uncontrollable pain that happened to you. Once you have thought through this with your brain, you can start to heal your heart. Healing in your mind and your heart are both necessary to move forward in this forgiving process.

I know I'm running the risk of losing you here, but this can be a vital part of the forgiveness process. A lot of us have issues with organized religion and, as a result, we also discount the possibility of a loving God's existence. It is impossible to generalize a process to analyze God's existence in a world filled with hardship, so I'll offer one small encouragement: Try!

Give yourself at least fifteen minutes to verbalize the frustrations of the uncontrollable hardships in your Yesterday. Shout out how you feel. I know this may seem odd, but do it and then stop and listen. Listen to your emotions, listen to your surroundings, take note of what you hear. Then think. Think about the world's design. Think about the sunrises and sunsets you have watched. Listen and think some more!

Don't forget that your Purpose Guide is here for you. We do not sit in judgment. Wrestling with God's existence amidst a broken world is a common factor in the human experience, so you can be sure that it's part of the fullest experience of your Renewal Journey.

Grab Your Journal

« Based on the low points of your life graph, where do you need to forgive God for how you perceived God did something to you or let something awful happen to you?

« Based on the low points of your career graph, where do you need to forgive God for how you perceived God did something to you or let something awful happen to you?

« What do the beauty and harmony of life tell you about restoring a broken world?

« What does living life in a broken world mean to you?

« How can you navigate it?

Guilt and Shame: Understanding Yesterday's Mistakes

Most of us have moments in our past that we regret: times when we were not who we wanted to be and times we acted outside our expectations for how we want to behave. During these times we may have hurt those we love or caused ourselves unwanted pain.

Processing the guilt I carried around was one of the most significant revelations on my life graph this past year. I had buried the memory of a lie I had told a good friend that went on to harm him and others. I had not consciously thought about it for a few years, but that relationship had gone stagnant due to my mistake. As I went through my life graph, that moment came back to me, and I worked through my emotions to realize it was time I forgive myself for that occurrence and seek to make things right with my old friend.

I set up a time to chat with my friend and formally apologized. I let him know how I did not mean to hurt him. He forgave me, and we are now friends again. After forgiving myself and mending the relationship, I learned some valuable lessons about guilt. When we hold onto guilt, it will keep us from our ability to connect with others. The guilt I was carrying created a sense of shame that was keeping me from being my best self.

Guilt is born from a behavior or event that you may regret. Shame is the way you feel about yourself, sometimes because of a feeling of guilt that you haven't acknowledged. It is essential to clarify the two because they must be dealt with differently.

For me, the lie I had told hindered the relationship with my old friend, but by not dealing with the guilt of that lie, I was subconsciously feeling like a liar. I am not a liar. I hold honesty as one of my core values, but after forgiving myself, I could see I was carrying the shame of being a liar due to that past, isolated event. I now felt free to be close to many other old friends whom I feared saw me as a liar. The guilt of that one lie turned to shame.

There are moments in your yesterday that have caused guilt. In dealing with these moments and forgiving yourself, you will alleviate some of the shame in your identity. Easing that shame will help you more deeply connect with those around you. You are not the product of your mistakes. Forgive yourself, break free from guilt, and heal any shame keeping you from being your best self!

Grab Your Journal

« Based on the low points of your life graph, do you need to forgive yourself for something you did that has caused you or someone else pain?

« Has this caused you a sense of shame about your identity?

« How can you reconstruct your identity?

« Based on the low points of your career graph, do you need to forgive yourself for something you did that has caused you or someone else pain?

« Has this caused you a sense of shame about your identity?

« How can you reconstruct your identity?

Resentment: Understanding Those Who Hurt You

If you are holding grudges from yesterday's hardships, it is time to address them. Resentment against those who have hurt you can have disastrous effects on your life and your identity. Owning resentment is essential to making sure you are safe during your Renewal Journey.

Forgiving others for the pain caused by their action is really hard! Let's get that out there. Why is it so hard to forgive and so easy to hold grudges? We often hold back forgiveness because we feel (consciously or unconsciously) that if we forgive, then the person who hurt us will be "winning." This mindset could not be further from the truth. Our inability to forgive others rarely causes them any burden but most always imprisons us.

Forgiveness is a process that looks different for different people with different hardships, but there are a few valuable generalities that can make the process more manageable. Consider this:

It is highly unlikely that your lack of forgiveness is going to teach others the lesson you wish they would learn. When we forgive others for their actions, however, it does not mean we abandon accountability. Accountability and boundaries are still necessary. Only you will know the right level of accountability to maintain healthy boundaries once forgiveness takes place, but it will be done with right intent only if there is a forgiving heart behind it.

Embracing forgiveness of our own mistakes is a good foundation for being able to forgive others. Once you go through the process of forgiving yourself, you will find it easier to accept the imperfection of others. You make mistakes. Others do too. This pattern helps us embrace a graceful posture. Grace, the act of getting what we do not deserve, is essential to forgiveness. When you let go of guilt for what you have done, you receive grace. Now, by forgiving others, you give grace to them.

"She doesn't deserve forgiveness. If I forgive her, it will let her off the hook."

This was what my friend Chad said as he processed the most

devastating hardships in his life. A previous fiancée had done a horrible thing to him, and it still lingered some five years later. He had not been the same since. He was aware of how awful it was and how it had changed his view of relationships. His resentment was keeping him in pain. He recognized the hardship, but he had not done the work of forgiving her.

As Chad and I embraced some of these lessons about grace, forgiveness, accountability, and the poor psychology of his resentment, he started to gain a better perspective. His shift to owning the grudge moved him to a place of wanting freedom from the resentment. We walked through that forgiveness journey together. The pain has not vanished for Chad, but he no longer is living with the burden of resentment. Chad is his old self again, full of life, laughter, and joy. The resentment he released gave him the freedom to remember his true identity.

Do not let what others have done to you limit your ability to obtain your Purpose Dreams. Take forgiveness of others seriously, and it will radically change you!

Grab Your Journal

- « Based on the low points of your life graph, do you need to forgive others for what they have done to you?
- « Based on the low points of your career graph, do you need to forgive others based on what they have done to you?
- « Who was leading you during the low points of your career? What was their leadership like? How did they manage you? Did you feel respected? If not, what would have shown you respect?

Eliminating Subconscious Enemies Lingering from Your Hardships

Recognizing and categorizing the hardships in your Yesterday is the foundational step toward forgiveness. Whether it is God, yourself, or others, now is the time to gain the right perspective. In some instances, you may need to go a step further to eliminate the emotional influences of guilt, shame, or resentment. These lingering threats are tough to overcome. It takes concrete action to own them.

While forgiveness will not erase the memory of the pain, it will free you to live in peace with its existence. You can move forward with the awareness that it no longer has power over you. Forgiveness can be a process. It is not just flipping a switch. It may take time. For now, realize the potential of forgiveness and stay committed to it.

Here are three activities that can help you forgive yourself or another.

Forgiveness Blessing

When others have hurt you, it is easy to get into a mode of wishing similar pain for them. If this resonates with you, this simple exercise can break that thought pattern and free up some of the negative energy you are spending so that you can use your energy more positively.

Think of people who have created pain in your life.

Think about what you hope happens to them.

Stop, and if those wishes are negative, take them back and try to start wishing good things for them.

Even if it is that you hope they change their ways and become better people, it is a positive wish to communicate about them. If it is more specific, convey that in your thoughts, but make sure you reframe any negative wish into a positive blessing.

It's OK if this doesn't feel genuine. For now it will help you recognize the negative energy you are spending on things out of your control. It can also help you gain freedom as you seek goodness as opposed to harm. Just try it! If it does not work, go on to the next exercise. If it does, keep it as a rhythm for life and then move on to the next exercise.

Forgiveness Meditation

Close your eyes and breathe deeply.

Reflect on the pain in your life you want to be healed.

Picture in your mind the incident in your life that hurts you the most.

Go back to the place, the time, and the event or person that hurt you so deeply.

See the look on his or her face. Hear the words that were spoken.

Live them again. Be in tune with your feelings as you replay this circumstance.

Now, in your meditation, acknowledge how you feel. If you are seeking forgiveness of another that hurt you, imagine telling that person of your hurt and resentment. Stick with "I feel..." statements, not with "you did..." statements. This will keep the sense of ownership on you and your emotions as opposed to giving them power over you with their actions.

See in your mind the look on the other person's face. See his or her pain, incomprehension, and sorrow.

Now with the awareness of how much you needed to do this, tell the other person that you do forgive him or her and that you let go of the hurt by forgiving them.

When you are ready, take a deep breath and open your eyes.

Forgiveness Letter

Just as we did in the meditation above, go back to the moment that caused you pain. As emotions and memories come forth, write a letter to this person or about this event. Explain how it made you feel. Focus on your feelings, not his or her actions. Write that it is time to be free from this pain. Write an expression of your forgiveness.

Conclude your letter and go to a safe place with the intent of burning the letter (fireplace, fire pit, over a bucket). Burn a side of the letter and recognize the freeing of that moment. Let it go and watch it vanish to ash.

Breathe, meditate, and release the hurt as the paper burns. Commit to marking that moment in some way.

Grab Your Journal

- « How have these exercises helped you heal from what you were holding onto?
- « How can you make forgiveness a more regular rhythm in your life?
- « Are there any hardships that you need to forgive yourself for?
- « Are there any hardships that you need to forgive others for?

Thank you for your courage to forgive. You have just given yourself a great gift: more freedom from your Yesterday hardships, Ownership of what you can control, and Understanding that will surpass all knowledge. If you are fostering any confusion, guilt, shame, or resentment, consider connecting to a Purpose Guide. We are trained to walk you through these tough-to-navigate emotions.

Through your deep dive and action toward forgiveness today, you have courageously lessened a severe threat to identifying your Purpose Dreams. With the proper categorization and the action to defeat the pain, guilt, shame, and resentment, you are now safely on the path toward your destination. You are headed in the right direction: toward your Purpose Dreams!

Gratitude

CASHEWS, DRIED PINEAPPLE, GRANOLA, sunflower seeds, chocolate—yes, please! Those long days of hiking in Costa Rica required many energy boosters, but none as crucial or delicious as our trail mix. Like an energy boost on a hard, strenuous climb, the people in your life propel you along your journey. When you realize how important they have been in light of your whole life journey, you discover that their influence is a big part of the person you have become.

Today, you get to take inventory of all the fantastic people who have influenced your Yesterday. Recognition of these relationships will bring you to a whole new level of understanding and ownership in your Renewal Journey.

The Attitude of Gratitude Will take You to a Whole New Latitude!

Career seekers tend to focus on what they want to gain in the future; however, right perspective can be the result of taking inventory in what you already have. Out of all you have been given, relationships are the greatest gift. To look ahead to your Purpose Dreams, you must look back, learn from those who have boosted you, and celebrate them.

Some of those you will be celebrating today will be obvious, but others will be those I call "Silent Giants." These are the people in your life who quietly and humbly modeled characteristics that you wanted to emulate. On most life and career graphs these Silent Giants are the ones who were not only there in the highest and lowest moments, but rather they stood by you through it all—highs, lows, and the ordinary times in between.

A posture of true gratitude gives us a healthier life. You can change your mental mindset by taking five minutes a day to recognize your gifts and be grateful for them. And you will discover that the greatest of those gifts is the people in your life.

Grab Your Journal

Questions to Explore on Your Life Graph

« Stop and give thanks for the mountaintop moments in your life.

« Who were you with? How should you thank them?

« Who set the stage for the high points in your life? How should you thank them?

« At the low points on your life graph, who was with you, helping you through? How should you thank them?

« Who are your Silent Giants, the ones who modeled the way you want to live? How should you thank them?

Questions to Explore on Your Career Graph

« Who was leading you at the high points of your career? What was their leadership like? How did they manage you? How should you thank them?

« Who helped lead you to the high points in your career? How should you thank them?

« In the low points of your career, who was with you, helping you through? How should you thank them?

« Who are your Silent Giants, the ones who modeled the way you want to work? How should you thank them?

True Gifts

In the weeks that led up to my birthday this past year, I decided to set aside some time every day to take inventory of my true gifts. One of the ways I did this was to go through my contacts on my phone, giving thanks for the people who had made me who I am. I texted and called dozens of people who had made an impact on my life and career. I told them how grateful I was for their selfless investment in my future. So many of those I spoke with were touched to know how much they had affected my journey.

Pure, unconditional love does not require a reward. Most of the people you reflect upon do not expect a thank you or a call to say how much they influenced your life. Few of the people you recognize for making a difference in your life will be on the news for their actions toward you. But you can repay their efforts by finding ways to encourage them now for the ways they made a difference in your life and career. The people you recognize are the true gifts in life.

Relational Treasure: Who Can I Impact?

One of the biggest game changers for me as I went through my life and career graphs a couple of years ago was when I realized I was spending way too much time working. I was chasing after some career ambitions that were exciting, yet keeping me from a work-life balance that allowed me to focus on the most important relationships in my life. I started to realize how many people I had not reached out to in a long time.

I preach "people before accomplishments" all the time to my kids, but in this season, I had subtly fallen away from what I knew to be true. I was not practicing what I preached. My performance idol had blinded me to the value of those treasured relationships.

"Where your treasure is, there your heart will also be." Your heart drives much of your mind and action. For me, I was treasuring career success over relationships. Once I realized this, I made some immediate changes. Since then, I've maintained a better work-life balance. I still work hard, but I no longer sacrifice valued relationships to the god of greater worldly success.

> **Grab Your Journal**
>
> « What do you treasure most?
> « Who do you treasure most?
> « Do your work obligations ever keep you from giving your "A" game to those you treasure the most?
> « Are there changes you need to make to ensure your actions mimic your treasure?

Relational Purpose: How Can I Impact?

Bad news constantly bombards us: shootings here, robberies there, lies everywhere. That is not where I want the focus of my life to be. Take ownership of where you focus your attention. Focus on the positive influences in your life.

At the root of our admiration and appreciation of those who have been important to us is a recognition of their goodness. We all want to have that same goodness and to be a positive influence on others. When you are making a positive impact, you will be more satisfied with your work. When you are more satisfied with your work, you will be more engaged. Part of the unlocking of your Purpose Dreams is understanding how you are designed to make a positive impact on people.

How you can make a positive influence on those in your life and career is your unique relational purpose. This does not mean we all need to work for a nonprofit organization or go into ministry.

We can all impact those around us by how we work, not just where we work or what we do. No matter what career calling you embrace, you can positively influence others.

Grab Your Journal

« Of those who impacted your career journey the most, what can you learn about how they worked?
« Is there someone in your life, right now, who you can impact positively? How might you do it?
« Make a plan and do it!
« Is there someone in your work, right now, who you can impact positively? How might you do it? Make a plan and do it!

Relational treasure is who is in your sphere of influence. Relational purpose is how you can impact those in your sphere of influence. Alignment of your relational treasure and your relational purpose is essential to finding your unique Purpose Dreams.

Grab Your Journal

« Who do you treasure for the positive impact they have made on your life?
« Who do you treasure for the positive impact they have made on your career?
« Who can you impact positively?
« How can you have a positive impact on those in your sphere of influence?
« What is getting in the way of that potential impact?

The unexpected combination of diverse ingredients in trail mix makes up a unified harmony. As you gain a new perspective and develop gratitude for the diverse mix of great people on your trail of life, seek to emulate the impact they had by influencing others. As you contemplate what it looks like to better align your relational treasure with your relational purpose, know that freedom and joy await. You are headed in the right direction: toward your Purpose Dreams!

Understanding Material Needs
and Wants

LYDIA IS OUR YOUNGEST CHILD. She is two years old and navigating her independence. She regularly falls prey to wanting what her brother and sister are playing with. She can be completely content with whatever she is playing with until she sees her older siblings enjoying something else. She then stomps over, in typical two-year-old style, ambitiously seeking that object of delight. Her desire to have what others have has landed her many quick stints in the timeout chair.

I hope we're more mature than a two-year-old when we consider our needs and wants. Many career seekers, though, lack self-awareness about their genuine needs and wants. Marketing messages around success and material consumption have affected our ability to define what we need and what we want. This is no way to live a purposeful life. If work is partially designed to help us obtain our needs and wants, then we need to be more intentional about what those are.

When we were on jungle trails for days at a time, we had to master bringing only necessary items. If you carry too much weight, you cannot sustain the physical rigors of the journey. You quickly discover how to get rid of those things that aren't essential.

Day-to-day life in America is a lot more forgiving. Over-packing your life with wants, rather than needs, seems to have few ramifications, but hidden effects are weighty indeed. The treadmills of disengagement are often full of great people trying to obtain wants that they have categorized as needs. Understanding needs while balancing the achievement of healthy wants is the combination we must seek. Understanding the balance comes first, followed by the discipline that will help us achieve that balance. One without the other will lead to misaligned priorities and the potential for chasing after Purpose Dreams that are not unique to you.

Today will be an opportunity for a personal timeout (no timeout chair necessary) to analyze whether you have poorly categorized your wants as needs. You will learn to be intentional about your wants and needs. The renewed awareness of material resources will sharpen your Purpose Dreams.

Rest assured, this analysis does not aim to turn you into a minimalist. It will help you define practical Purpose Dreams that will meet all your material needs, your healthy wants, and give you purpose, freedom, and joy.

Being Rich!

Have you ever thought about what it means to be rich?

Most of us tend to think that being rich is associated with how much money we have in the bank. On my journey to Costa Rica, I learned another way to look at riches and, in fact, it might have given me the perspective on what true riches are. The Costa Rican people, known as *Ticos*, live a communal life, reliant on one another to sustain themselves. They seemed content even in the midst of adversity; they had an inner peace that kept hardship from stealing their joy. Their motivation was profound, yet straightforward: Focus on the goodness of family and neighbors. They did not have much money or many material possessions, but it was hard not to want what they had. It seemed to me they were rich in all the things that truly matter!

The *Ticos's* way of life taught me that there are four areas of riches in life: material, relational, motivational, and spiritual. Over the next four days of your Renewal Journey, we will be exploring all four areas. This analysis will help you identify the right success factors for your career path. Please trust the process and give it serious thought; I assure you it will make your path straight! When we have a more balanced approach to the resources we need and want in our lives, we will develop more fulfilling Purpose Dreams. We walk into our purpose free of burdens and rich in joy!

Needs vs. Wants

Every year, my loved ones ask the same question: "What do you want for your birthday?" At this point in my life, there is not much I want that I do not already have, so I usually reframe that question to let them know what I need. This year it's a needle-nose plier, sports socks, and jasmine green tea. I'm a pretty wild guy!

Wants are not inherently dangerous. Wants are not a deterrent to happiness unless we wrap our identity up in them. Then they become idols and do not serve our best self. It is essential to have healthy wants and strive toward obtaining those wants as long as we take into consideration all four areas of our wants and needs (material, relational, motivational, and spiritual).

I have seen many career seekers let wants trump their needs. A holistic view of wants and needs is helpful to crafting a good career-seeking strategy. It is essential to defining and achieving your Purpose Dreams. By the end of today, you will know the difference between your wants and your needs. This will help you keep your eyes on the right prize.

Let's begin with this question:

Is your identity wrapped up in the pursuit of any of your wants?

Please don't let the answer to this question shame you. This part of the journey is all about having self-awareness of what drives your ambition. When you analyze your wants, consider whether these wants can bring you or others genuine and lasting joy. If they can, they may be healthy, so don't abandon them too quickly. Here are some further questions to help you analyze your wants.

Grab Your Journal

« How will your wants impact your relationships?

« How will your wants influence your health?

« How will your wants influence your Purpose Dreams?

You have unique needs and wants. Do not let anyone else tell you what to strive for. Free yourself from external pressures and definitions of success. Rich purpose, rich freedom, and a rich pursuit of joy await as you construct your needs and wants!

Material Needs

Today we will focus on the first of the four needs in our life: material needs. We have all heard the saying, "Money is the root of all evil." Few of us believe this. But the reality is that greed—an excessive craving for material wealth—can lead us away from the proper use of money to meet our real needs.

I had a season of my life where I was unconscious of my desire for excessive wealth. Our business was thriving. Material wealth came easy. But I let this material wealth have power over my needs and healthy wants. This season was a great teacher for me. It taught me that more wealth could create more problems. I spent more time trying to create even more wealth. I regretfully recall explaining to my wife that I needed to work more to "strike while the iron was hot." That took more of my time away from my family and eventually led to some unhealthy relational rifts. I also became physically unhealthy. I slept less, exercised less, ate more fast food, and put on weight. I became less mentally healthy. I was less well-rounded and had tunnel vision toward my greedy ambitions. This kept me from activities that I enjoy to maintain my mental health. I am not proud of that season, but recognizing its pitfalls helped me grow in wisdom.

Grab Your Journal

Questions to Explore about Your Material Needs and Wants

« Have there been any times when you have been overly ambitious about gathering excessive material wealth?

« How did it affect your deepest relationships?

« How did it affect your physical health?

« How did it affect your mental health?

« How did it affect your career path?

« How can you recognize this behavior in the future to make sure you do not fall prey to this faulty mindset?

Material Needs Analysis

Typically when a job seeker considers his or her material needs, a lot of assumptions are made. Surprisingly, most job seekers do not analyze their material needs. Most believe they need to earn what they are accustomed to because they based their lifestyle on that amount. Let's gain clarity to confirm or debunk that assumption for you today.

There are many models of financial planning, and it is not within the scope of this journey to recommend any specific method. We do believe firmly in this general goal: 80 percent of income to live; 10 percent to save; 10 percent to give to a cause important to you.

Our family has found this model useful. When we earn more than what we have budgeted, then my wife and I look at that excess and determine together where we should invest it: in savings/investment, in giving, or in a purchase aligned with our healthy wants.

So, get out your checkbook or log in to your bank account online, and let's start charting your financial needs. You will want to get your last four months' spending habits to get a good average of each month. If there is a spouse or another family member involved in the financial decisions, you will want to do this with him or her to ensure you are both on the same page about needs and wants. There will be some additional layers to these categories if you have children, but generally, you will still be able to group your financial needs for them in one of these categories.

Living Situation

« *What are you currently spending per month on your living situation (including all rents, mortgage, utilities, etc...)?*

$ _____

« *Are there any changes needed in your current living situation?*

A. **TOTAL monthly earning needed to cover Living Situation:**

$ _____

Food

« *What are you currently spending per month on food?*

$ _____

« *Are there changes needed in the amount you are spending on food?*

B. **TOTAL monthly earning needed to cover Food:**

$ _____

Clothes

« *What are you currently spending per month on clothes?*

$ _____

« *Are there changes needed in the amount you are spending on clothes?*

C. **TOTAL monthly earning needed to cover Clothes:**

$ _____

Health and Wellness

« *What are you currently spending per month on activity associated with health (nonfood related)?*

$ _____

« *Are there changes needed tin the amount you are spending on health and wellness?*

D. **TOTAL monthly earning needed to cover Health and Wellness:** $ _____

Personal Development

« *What are you currently spending per month on activity associated with personal development?*

$ _____

« *Are there changes needed in the amount of money you are spending on personal development?*

E. **TOTAL monthly earning needed to cover Personal Development:**

$ _____

Transportation / Auto

« *What are you currently spending per month on your automobile / transportation?*

$ _____

« *Are there any changes needed in your transportation costs?*

F.   **TOTAL monthly earning needed to cover Transportation:**

$ _____

Generosity

« *What are you currently giving to those in need per month?*

$ _____

« *Are there changes needed in the amount you are giving?*

G.   **TOTAL monthly earning needed to cover Generosity:**

$ _____

Saving

« *What are you currently saving per month?*

$ _____

« *Are there changes needed in the amount of money you are saving?*

H.   **TOTAL monthly earning needed to cover Savings:**

$ _____

Miscellaneous Costs

« *What are any miscellaneous costs not listed above?*

$ _____

« *Are there changes needed in the amount of money you are spending on any of these costs?*

I. TOTAL monthly earning needed to cover Miscellaneous
   Costs: $ _____

Rest / Vacation
   « *What are you currently spending per month on activities*
   that truly refuel you?
   $ _____
   « *Are there changes needed in the amount of money you are*
   spending on rest / vacation?
J. TOTAL monthly earning needed to cover Rest / Vacation:
   $ _____

Habits / Pleasures
   « *What are you currently spending per month on habits or*
   leisure activities?
   $ _____
   « *Are there changes needed in the amount of money you are*
   spending on leisure?
K. TOTAL monthly earning needed to cover Habits / Pleasures:
   $ _____

ADD IT ALL UP!
1. How much do you need to make per month to cover all of
   your expenses (SUM of A-K)?
   $ _____

Financial Analysis of Wants
An analysis of your wants and the health of those wants are key
to determining your Purpose Dreams. Take some time now to
discover how your wants fit into your current needs.

« *What are some things or activities that you may want in the future?*

« *Are these wants essential to your identity?*

« *Are these wants adding value to your life, your wellness, or your relationships?*

« *Based on our previous analysis of wants, would you categorize these as healthy wants?*

« *What are some healthy wants that you will need to plan for financially?*

« *To be achieved in two years:* _____

_____

« *To be achieved in five years:* _____

_____

2. **How much do you need to save today to afford these wants in two years?**

   $ _____

3. **How much do you need to save today to afford these wants in five years?**

   $ _____

Monthly Income Needed (SUM of 1-3): $ _____

This monthly income goal is a MUST when finding your new career role. It will provide for your healthy needs and help you work toward your healthy wants: A perfect balance!

This is a simplified way to get to the material needs and wants income goal. The more detail you can bring to your spending habits, the more awareness you will receive from the analysis. The more self-awareness you gain about your material needs and wants, the more clarity you will have about your Purpose Dreams. Don't let money have the power over your career dreams. Money's power is not intended to enslave you, but rather free you.

If this is a tough analysis for you, your Purpose Guide is well equipped to walk into this exercise with you. We are excited to see you gain career and life freedom through this analysis of your material needs and wants.

The journey in Costa Rica taught me to understand and own the right perspective on my needs and healthy wants. There are things I needed in my backpack to survive. I could not under pack, yet I could not afford to over pack, or I would be bogged down and unable to make the journey effectively. The same is true for you amidst your Renewal Journey. Don't under pack and don't over pack. Anything less than the right balance could lead your Renewal Journey down the wrong path.

Developing the correct Understanding and the right balance of needs and wants is critical to obtaining a career of purpose, freedom and joy. You are headed in the right direction: toward your Purpose Dreams!

Understanding Relational Impact

"ARE YOU KIDDING ME? YOU HAVE got to go, man!"

This animated conviction came from my friend Sam as we packed up camp. It was just a few months before my trip to Costa Rica. Sam and my other trail buddies encouraged me to take this life-changing adventure. My trail buddies were guys that I've known from different aspects of my life. We loved to break away from our fast-paced lives and go off into the woods for a long weekend. We formed deep and intimate friendships around campfires and during rock climbing journeys. Those guys knew me well, and because they genuinely cared, they were in a unique position to encourage me. They wanted what was best for me, so their perspective has been profound in my journey through life.

In the same way, you have an impact on many people in your life. You are someone's trail buddy. The genuine care, encouragement, and feedback you give to those who trust you will influence their life decisions. This is a privilege and a blessing!

I have spent a lot of time with my trail buddies. When I get away with them, I can count on quality time with great perspective, fun, and an environment of love. This did not come right away. I have nurtured those relationships. You cannot have quality time with great friends if you do not also invest a quantity of time. Time is needed to develop deep and trusting relationships. Relational abundance requires investment.

ROI: The Metric of all Metrics

Return on Investment, ROI, is the most important metric for business and investment success. As we have discovered, financial prowess is just one of the four variables in our needs. The most important of our needs and wants are relational. Recall the depth of Day Two and Day Three on our retreat journey. Chances are the highest and lowest points on your career and life graphs had more to do with your relationships than they did your material wealth. As we explore relational impact, let me give you a definition for relational ROI: Return on Involvement.

Relational ROI can pay great dividends and lead to a full life of liberty and happiness. The healthier our relationships are, the more effective we're going to be in all aspects of our lives. The pursuit of excessive material riches often deters relational wealth. Most billionaires regret the relational sacrifices they made to achieve their status of material wealth. Finding your balance of material and relational wealth is a key to sustaining happiness in your life.

As you make your way through today's exercises, take pride in how you impact those around you. Part of your purpose is relative to who you impact. Downplaying your role in the lives of those closest to you will not lead you to full Purpose Dreams. Your involvement in others' lives is an investment with significant returns.

Setting boundaries in your career that will allow you to spend the right quantity of time with friends and family will lead to quality relationships. Running after success factors that do not consider your relational investments will likely lead you to disengagement.

Quality relationships do not come without investment. Good relational investments do not happen by accident. It takes a lot of intentionality, grace, and truth to develop them. The stories and exercises ahead will help you explore both quality and quantity time with those you love. What you learn today will help you draft your Purpose Dreams with the confidence that you will be investing in others as well as yourself.

Scroll back to your notes from Day Four when you celebrated all the people who have invested their time and energy in you. You are evidence of the return on their involvement. Now, it is time to understand how your investment in others can have good relational ROI.

Grab Your Journal

« Who do you want to see live joy-filled lives?

« How can you give them quality time to impact their journey?

« What lessons from your own journey will give you wisdom to share with them?

« Have others recently told you they were struggling in a particular area of life where you might be able to help?

« What can you offer to positively impact their journey?

« What lessons may you be positioned to help them with due to your own journey?

« As you have and continue to uncover greater self-awareness on your retreat journey, is there anyone who might benefit from what you are learning? Map out a plan to share with them what you've learned.

ROI: Their Needs Are Unique too!

As you craft your Purpose Dreams through your Renewal Journey, be aware that your needs and wants may not be the same for those around you. Do your best not to project what you are learning onto others. Our loved ones have their own needs and wants that may not align with yours. Crafting Purpose Dreams without that awareness may not give you the Relational ROI you desire.

This understanding came to light for me with the brilliant teaching of Dr. Gary Chapman, author of *The Five Love Languages*. Dr. Chapman says we all have love tanks, and we yearn for them to be filled by those we love. Loving others the way we feel loved may not fill their love tank. The five love languages are acts of service, physical touch, words of affirmation, quality time, and gifts. Understanding these love languages (and applying them) has been foundational in my marriage, but I now see their merit in all of my most important relationships.

Early in our marriage, my wife had a tough day. She is a school teacher and an unusual event with one of the students brought her much stress. As she tearfully shared with me the circumstance, I wanted to support and love her the best I could. After she calmed down, I drew her a bath and told her to relax while I made dinner. I ran out to the grocery store, picked up flowers and ingredients for dinner, and came home to prepare it. When she came down from her bath, she was surprised to see what I had prepared. The flowers, the food, and the attention to detail I had given to this meal were impressive—at least to me.

I feel loved through acts of service and receiving gifts. My wife's love language involves words of affirmation and physical touch. I was loving her the way I like to be loved. She would have felt more loved if I had given her a back rub while affirming her in the way she was handling the situation at school. Because I was not speaking her love languages, my well-intended investment of time and love in her did not have the impact that I had hoped.

To ensure true Relational ROI, you will want to be aware of others' love languages and how you can make the most impact. I would encourage you to explore the five love languages at http://www.5lovelanguages.com/. On this site, you can take a short, free quiz to unlock awareness about your predominant love languages. Your loved ones can do the same. Being aware of the different love languages can be a game changer in the way you love those that you are called to impact in life.

Grab Your Journal

Has there ever been a situation where you have gone to great lengths to help or love someone you cared about, but it did not have the impact you imagined?

ROI: Their Success Factors Are Unique, too!

Keith and I go way back. He recently sought my guidance to help his brother, Tim, develop a more meaningful career path. I also knew Tim well, and after the conversation with Keith, I had the opportunity to ask him about how he was doing. It turns out Tim was doing very well. He didn't have the flashy toys or the level of worldly success Keith possessed, but he was happy and more engaged in his career purpose than Keith was. Keith had genuine concern for Tim. He thought helping him gain more worldly success would make him more fulfilled. That was a poor assumption. It is commonplace to make assumptions for those we love the most about how they could be successful. In doing so, we are projecting our success factors on them. Awareness of projecting your success factors on anyone you love (and resisting the urge to do it!) will enhance your ROI.

Grab Your Journal

« Fill in the blanks:

« I think _____'s life would be better if he
or she _____.

« Is that desire for the person based on your needs and
wants?

« Is that assumption healthy?

« Is that assumption based on fact?

As you find your Purpose Dreams, don't assume everyone should view success the way you do.

ROI: Don't Assume. Communicate!

Your definition of your needs, wants, and success factors may impact the journey of those closest to you. If you are married or have dependents, their well-being could be affected by the way you determine your needs and wants. We need to have accountability with those we love the most. I've learned this in my marriage. I need to communicate my Purpose Dreams to my wife, and we need to agree to them together. This kind of communication can be complicated. It's not exactly a favorite topic for date night. As my wife and I have learned to get on the same page, though, we have minimized assumptions about each other's needs, wants, and success factors. We can now successfully craft one vision for our individual and collective paths toward a family Purpose Dream.

As you uncover your needs, wants, and success factors, don't assume that others need what you need. If your Purpose Dreams will impact any of your relationships, communicate what you are finding to that person. I assure you the ROI will be profound.

> **Grab Your Journal**
>
> « Is there anyone who is impacted by your definition of needs and wants?
>
> « Is there anyone who is reliant on you for the fulfillment of his or her needs or wants?

As you consider those closest to you and how you can have great relational ROI, you are gaining self-awareness to align your relational treasures with your relational purpose. The return on your relational investment will be life-changing, for you and all those you impact!

As you conclude your contemplation on relational needs, here are a few more questions to help you determine the right boundaries.

> **Grab Your Journal**
>
> « Am I a good son or daughter?
>
> « Am I a good friend?
>
> « Am I a good spouse (if applicable)?
>
> « Am I a good parent (if applicable)?
>
> « Am I a good citizen?
>
> « Am I making this world a better place for others to live in?

Now, put all you have examined together as you configure your relational needs relative to your Purpose Dreams.

> **Grab Your Journal**
>
> *Questions to Explore about Your Relational Needs*
> « Who do you want to see live joy-filled lives?
> « How can you give them the right quantity of quality time?
> « Is there anyone you need to communicate with about what you are discovering during your exploration of needs and wants?
> « List a few boundaries you need in your career to ensure you have Relational ROI.

Life is a journey. It is a blessing to have great trail buddies along for the trek. Your Purpose Dreams will become reality when you obtain a career and life with boundaries that keep you investing wisely into the lives of your trail buddies. As you near the destination of obtaining a career according to your Purpose Dreams, set the right boundaries. You are headed in the right direction: toward your Purpose Dreams!

Understanding Motivational Boundaries

"DO NOT TOUCH OR EAT FROM THE manchineel tree!" This was a familiar warning from our guides in Costa Rica. The manchineel tree is considered one of earth's most poisonous trees. Its little, green, apple-like fruit appeals to the eye and the appetite, but don't be fooled. The fruit will taste sweet at first, but the toxic effects then wreak havoc on the body.

Much like that fruit, the career motivations of many Americans have toxic effects on their happiness. At first glance, being ambitious to do your best and obtain the most material gain does not seem bad, yet without a greater awareness of your real needs and wants, your motivations may prove poisonous.

Today, we will take a look at our motivations to ensure they are in line with the life we want to live. As you near the destination of your Purpose Dreams, let's further define some of the pressures and temptations that we face when seeking a career of purpose.

Motivation and Temptation

What has motivated you to become who you have become?

The answers to this crucial question will help you determine healthy motivations as well as create boundaries to avoid unhealthy temptations. Two key factors often creep into our motivation: One is the opinions and expectations of those we love; the other is the temptations that are commonplace in our society.

The Family of Origin Motivation

I passed the box of tissues to my friend Tom as he wept. We were processing the closure of his small business venture. Tom had been a teacher straight out of college and always excelled in that environment. Teaching was his true gift and purpose, but a few years earlier, Tom had decided to quit his teaching career in favor of launching an entrepreneurial business venture. His business idea had some potential, but Tom was not built to be an entrepreneur; he was created to be an excellent teacher.

As we explored the emotions he was having about this "failure," we finally got to the root of the issue at hand: Why did he leave his sweet spot of teaching? His answer revealed a truth that motivates many of us.

Tom had come from a large family of business practitioners. Most had been successful on the world's terms and had accumulated much material wealth and business prowess. As a result, Tom grew up in a family with an affluent lifestyle. He followed his heart to find his passion for teaching, but after years of doing what he loved, he felt he needed to "live up to" his family's success in business. The major influence in his decision to start a business had everything to do with the fact that, subconsciously, his view of success had been conditioned by his family of origin.

As we started to reveal these truths together, Tom said, "I realized I was chasing an idol of success incongruent with my purpose." Bingo!

The perception of success in Tom's family created norms that Tom felt he needed to strive for. These norms had been driving him away from his life's purpose.

If family-of-origin expectations are part of your success factors, you will need to deeply analyze where they came from and what they mean to you. You are not your brother, your sister, your mother, or your father. You do not need to fill anyone's shoes but your own. Family norms are real, and identifying them can free you to be your awesome self!

Often family expectations will be perceived, not directly communicated. Maybe you grew up observing someone you saw as successful. Somewhere along the way, you adopted his or her success factors and Purpose Dreams. Chasing after someone else's Purpose Dreams is sure to keep you on your treadmill of disengagement.

Grab Your Journal

« What did success look like to your father?

« Is his view of success relevant to your view of success?

« What did success look like to your mother?

« Is her view of success relevant to your view of success?

« As you look back at your family of origin, are there any expectations of success that you are trying to meet?

Throughout my years walking career seekers to Purpose Dreams, family-of-origin motivators almost always have played a role in chasing wrong dreams. Capturing the truth of who you were made to be, regardless of the perception of success of those you grew up with, is vital at this stage of your Renewal Journey. Take the time necessary to forgive or heal from anything you might be uncovering.

Your family of origin and your Yesterday experiences have real power over you unless you are aware of their potentially toxic presence. In the same way, the world you live in promotes ideals of happiness and success that can keep you from being the best version of yourself. Allowing these temptations to drive your success factors and Purpose Dreams is dangerous.

Worldly Temptations

Being aware of my temptations has been and continues to be crucial for me to sustain healthy motivational boundaries. It is not easy, but well worth the fight. When I lack awareness, these temptations have power to keep me from my best self. The three most common temptations that creep into my life are pleasure, pride, and power. These tempting motivators are not unique to me. I find they drive many of us toward a version of success that is not best serving ourselves or those around us.

Pleasure

There is nothing inherently wrong with pleasure. However, like most good things in life, pleasure in excess can have toxic effects. Your analysis today of which pleasures in your life are healthy or unhealthy will help you define boundaries that will keep you on the path to your Purpose Dreams. Distinguishing between healthy and unhealthy pleasures is the foundation to having control over any temptation from too much pleasure.

Grab Your Journal

« What gives you pleasure?

« Does this pleasure have any potential for personal negative impact?

« Does this pleasure have negative relational impact on those around me?

« What pleasures in your life are not serving your best self?

« What things do you enjoy that have a pattern of causing relational rifts?

« Could any pleasures be motivating you toward career ambitions not aligned with your unique purpose?

Admittedly, I have sometimes failed to stop and analyze pleasure in this way, but this discipline has been a game changer in ensuring that pleasure is not enslaving me. We all battle against unhealthy pleasure temptations. Take control of them! Become more self-aware today, and develop a plan to turn unhealthy pleasures into healthy boundaries. The Purpose Dreams that follow this discipline will bring you sustaining happiness!

Pride

I struggle with the temptation of pride. Many times in my career I have let success overpower my true identity. Being proud of accomplishments is healthy, but throughout my life, I have allowed those accomplishments to define my worth. I enjoy acknowledgment of my accomplishments. That is not always unhealthy, but seeking this acknowledgment has led to an unhealthy pride.

On my retreat journey, the temptation of pride leaped out from my graphs into my heart. As I looked at the lower points of my life, asking what was driving my dissatisfaction, I realized that I was trying to portray myself as someone I was not. This was driving behaviors and decision-making that had taken me down the wrong path. I was wearing a mask of accomplishment to cover up who I truly was. I was letting my desire of others' acceptance fuel pride. I may have felt accepted by others, yet deep down I knew it was a lie.

We all have worn masks to protect us from revealing our true self to a person or group we want to impress. We all seek approval on some level, but when the desire for approval keeps us from our best selves, we need to take another look at how important it is.

An analysis of your life and career graphs can reveal the masks you have worn throughout your life and career. Identifying these masks can help you break down the walls that keep you from your true self. This is one way I have worked on my pride.

Do not be shamed by the past masks you have worn. The revelation of why you have worn these masks is the power you need to destroy them. The freedom to enjoy your true identity will launch you toward your Purpose Dreams!

Grab Your Journal

« On your best days, who do you tell about your joy?

« On your worst days, who do you go to?

« In the highest points of your career, who did you seek to tell about your "success"?

« In the lowest points of your career, who were you afraid would find out about your "perceived failure"?

« Who is your audience?

« Who are you trying to please?

« What masks do you wear to impress others?

« How can you destroy these masks and be free to enjoy your true identity?

Power

Power has been a significant temptation on my journey. When I was a young and immature business leader, I had no one to hold me accountable. As I studied my career graph under the Costa Rica sun, I started to realize that I was becoming addicted to power. I am, by nature, an independent guy. This independence mixed with early business "success" slowly propelled me toward becoming a control freak. When I am unaware, this controlling nature can tempt me to an unhealthy idol of power.

I regret that I let the power of success and achievement jade my view of what is most important in my life. The mixture of my temptations toward power and pride has created an attitude of self-righteousness. This self-righteousness has hurt others. Daily, I need to reflect on my actions and behaviors to ensure that I'm not letting power motivate me. I must take those pride- and power-based thoughts captive to ensure they do not enslave me.

I'm thankful that my retreat journeys have led me to identify my temptations. I am not proud of how pleasure, pride, and power have influenced my journey; however, awareness of their impact has helped me calibrate my motivations to align with my best Purpose Dreams.

Grab Your Journal

« Have you conquered any past temptations that kept you from the best version of your life?

« If so, congrats! How did you keep them from creeping back into your life?

« Has power ever tempted you?

« Are you in control of your life?

At the beginning of this retreat day you looked at this question:

What has motivated you to become who you have become?

Now that you have analyzed some motivators, how might you better answer this question?

As you are taking control of your temptations and uncovering your motivators, dream of your new motivational riches as you explore this more relevant question:

What motivates you to be who you want to be?

Notice the difference in your answers to these last two questions. With awareness of unhealthy motivations, you will craft healthy motivational boundaries. These boundaries will lead to freedom and new, profound Purpose Dreams.

Grab Your Journal

Take a Fresh Look at These Questions

« As you look back at your family of origin, are there any expectations of success that you are trying to meet?

« Could any pleasures be motivating you toward career ambitions not aligned with your unique purpose?

« Is trying to impress some person or group keeping you from your true purpose?

« What temptations do you need to be aware of when crafting your Purpose Dreams?

« What motivates you to be who you want to be?

« What top three temptations do you need to be aware of to ensure you are motivated by the right priorities in your life?

As you end today's analysis on your motivational boundaries, be reminded that eating the right fruit from the right tree will make all the difference. Today's exploration has helped you identify the right motivational boundaries essential to finding a fulfilling career. You are headed in the right direction: toward your Purpose Dreams!

Understanding Spiritual Needs

"GRAB ME THOSE BINOCULARS," I blurted out at Kristin. You had to be quick when spotting colorful birds in the Costa Rican rainforest. The binoculars heightened my joy in these moments. They helped us see, with greater precision, the perfect design of the creatures before us. Journeying through such an impressive ecosystem helped me realize I was part of a marvelous creation. It was easy to see the wonder of creation and have respect for its creator in the rainforest. It can be more challenging to gaze with the same wonder at our daily grind. How we look at the created world around us is closely tied to the way we view the Creator of the universe. Awareness of this perception and belief is essential to defining your Purpose Dreams.

Everyone has spiritual needs. Notice I did not say religious needs. Spirituality is different than religion. I write from a Christian perspective. If you have a different tradition or you are still seeking your spiritual home, know that you can still achieve your Purpose Dream. All I ask is that you be open to what I share here. Today you will pick up your binoculars and gain greater perspective as you marvel at creation and discover more about your spirituality.

Regardless of your past spiritual journey, it is essential to explore creation, your Creator, and how you fit in relationship with this

Higher Power. What you believe spiritually and how you connect with the divine elements of life is at the core of your decisions about how to live your best life.

This may be a comfortable topic for you. If that is the case, let's dig deeper. You will find additional reflections on this topic in *The Purpose Promise Workbook*. This may be an uncomfortable topic for you. If that is the case, don't abandon this part of the journey. The day ahead provides healthy boundaries for exploring your spiritual needs. Investing your whole self in this day of the Renewal Journey is vital for you to identify your Purpose Dreams.

Life's intricacies and beauty are inspiring. If you contemplate the whole of creation, it should not take you long to realize that you are not the center of the story. There is a design beyond you and a designer of all of creation. This thought alone will help spark your spiritual journey. Life is not all about you, but you are designed to walk in tandem with the Creator of life. Your Purpose Guide is here to support you on this intimate day of your retreat should you want a companion on this journey.

To craft your Purpose Dreams you must consider your spiritual needs. If you embark on a career path that leaves no room for time contemplating the great spiritual questions, you run the risk of being disengaged and unhappy. The spiritual side of your life needs to be nurtured.

Grab Your Journal

« Take a minute to look around you.

« Notice the design and detail of life.

« Recognize at least three perfectly made parts of creation.

« What does the design of those things say about your ideas of the Creator of all that is?

« What do you believe about the role the Creator of the universe plays in your life?

« How does your purpose in life and in your career relate to this Creator?

The One Who Created You Loves You

When most of us start exploring our spiritual beliefs, we tend to seek out wisdom about the identity of the Creator of the universe, commonly called God. This Creator is the great unknown, so this is a natural starting point; we want to fit God in a box that we understand. The more foundational exploration, however, might be considering how the Creator sees you. Once you have the right perspective of how your maker relates to you, you will be more effective in the way you can relate to your maker.

Answer this question as honestly as possible:

Do you believe that God loves you?

If that question doesn't resonate with you, try this one:

Do you believe in a benevolent universe? Do you believe that there is a higher power out there that wants what is good for you?

This is the fundamental question when exploring your relationship with God. To embrace your answer start with the logic of this retreat journey. Look at your life and career graph. Think back to the days of your retreat and the many material and relational gifts you celebrated. Look at the evidence.

Think about those you love. Why do you give them gifts?

What do the material and relational gifts, that are freely given to you, say about God's love for you?

When we look at the evidence of how we love others in our life and take inventory of the many gifts given by God, the picture of how much God loves us becomes much more transparent. Seek first this wisdom and all other answers will be added to your spiritual journey.

When your self-worth is rooted in the awareness of God's love for you, it changes your perspective on everything. Some of the many lies that the world throws at you and the subconscious nature of self-deception will dissipate as you gain this right perspective about how God loves you.

What Does Death Teach Us about Life?

We can learn a great deal about life from those nearing death. One of the most common lessons learned is that all the money they had in the bank, or the toys they had acquired, meant nothing. It was the memories, the relationships, the accomplishments, and the legacy that they valued in those final days. There is profound wisdom in this shared experience. Although most of us do not want to think about our mortality, it plays a big part in how we should live.

Simply put: A healthy exploration of death leads to a richer life!

I was contemplating this recently as I went to a friend's funeral. It was a hard day, and my friend was taken way too young, but I was struck by the eulogy. A family member addressed my friend's great legacy, the positive role he played in the lives of so many people, and the many ways he left the world a much better place.

That night I started to think about my eulogy. What would be said at my funeral? What did I want to be remembered for? Who did I want to impact? What legacy would I leave? These questions can give us a great deal of insight into the way we view life, death, God, and the purpose of our lives.

Have you ever considered these questions? Doing so can help you be more in tune with your spiritual needs. It may not be comfortable, but it is essential. Most of us fear dying, but our greater fear should be not living. When we do these exercises, we stop worrying about dying because we're focused on how we want to live. Here are some questions that can help further your spiritual journey.

> **Grab Your Journal**
>
> « What will your loved ones remember you for?
> « What legacy will you leave behind for those you love?
> « Who do you want to impact?
> « Who can you truly trust?
> « How do you cope with the fact that we are all going to die?

During the past four days, you have been exploring all the ways you can be rich: materially, relationally, motivationally, and spiritually. Take time today to reflect on where these riches in your life have come from and how grateful you are for those riches.

Who has provided you these riches?

As you engage in your spiritual journey, analyzing the source of your provision will lead you to an understanding of the loving and providential nature of the Creator, commonly referred to as God. As you take inventory of your riches, feel blessed and give thanks! God loves you. Feeling and believing in that love is a foundation of spiritual wealth that nobody can steal.

Remember to use your metaphorical binoculars to see the wonder and design that is beyond any human power to achieve. Let go of trying to make everything happen on your own. Accept God's love for you. Seeing God and yourself through the right lens will unleash a new and greater perspective that will lead you to your real purpose.

As we wrap up Day Eight of our Renewal Journey, take some time to examine what you've learned in the last four days. Dig in and spend time formulating detailed reponses to these questions. Don't forget to contact your Purpose Guide if you need some help, at www.purposepromise.org/tools. Your destination is just over the horizon!

Grab Your Journal

« During the higher times of your life, how were you being provided for:
  - « *Materially:*
  - « *Relationally:*
  - « *Motivationally:*
  - « *Spiritually:*
« During the lower times of your life, how were you being provided for:
  - « *Materially:*
  - « *Relationally:*
  - « *Motivationally:*
  - « *Spiritually:*
« During the higher times of your career, how were you being provided for:
  - « *Materially:*
  - « *Relationally:*
  - « *Motivationally:*
  - « *Spiritually:*

« During the lower times of your career, how were you being provided for:

« *Materially:*

« *Relationally:*

« *Motivationally:*

« *Spiritually:*

« What boundaries can help you prioritize the spiritual side of your life and your relationship with God?

Your Purpose Dreams

"THERE IT IS!" SHOUTED KRISTIN, AS we set our sights on the cleared, flat land designated for the retreat center. On day nine of our Costa Rican trek, we had reached our desired destination. After celebrating the success of reaching our destination, I grabbed my journal to capture the depth of the moment:

> "We made it! The journey through the forest has been intense, but today that intensity is brought into focus. The struggles, fears, and richness of our trek have brought me to a new perspective. Today, we have reached our physical destination, yet through this journey, I have reached new heights. I now know myself. I am aware of my past, my fears, my treasures, my pride, and my purpose. I no longer will be motivated by the dreams of others. I have new dreams. I am a new man!"

Day nine of my retreat journey was a day to summarize my learning and to formulate a plan. I was determined to keep that heightened state of awareness. I would be returning home the next day. I needed to change the way I lived there. I was not made to run on a treadmill of disengagement. I was not built to chase after other people's dreams. I was made *on* purpose, *for* a purpose, and living out that purpose was the plan I would create on Day Nine of my retreat.

Today, on your Day Nine, you will define your Purpose Dreams based on the previous eight days of your retreat. Your clearly defined Purpose Dreams will drive your career-seeking strategy. From your Purpose Dreams, you will develop metrics to guide you and clarify your goals. These metrics are your success qualifiers. Defining them will conclude the A-to-M portion of your career-seeking process and launch you into the N-to-Z portion so you can find the career of your dreams.

Terms of Engagement

I fondly remember when I knew I was going to make my longtime girlfriend, Julie, my wife. The process of finding the right partner in life starts with individual awareness. Once I dated my wife, it was clear she was perfect for me. We both had a good idea of who we were before we defined what we wanted out of a life partner. The process of fulfilling your Purpose Dreams has many similarities to the search for the right marriage partner. You now have the individual awareness of your goals and desires to begin to choose your right career suitor.

Today you will be compiling a one-page document detailing your success qualifiers. To create this document, you will distill all that you've learned on this Renewal Journey. This one-pager is your Purpose Dream Analysis, the outcome of the A-to-M career-seeking process. It contains the individual awareness necessary to find the right employer and fulfill your Purpose Dreams.

The N-to-Z of the career-seeking process is going to be much more efficient with the individual awareness you have acquired. Your Purpose Dream Analysis will have three parts: Your Sweet Spot Analysis, Your Motivational Reminder, and Your Priority

Buckets. Together, these areas will reveal exactly how you should navigate finding the right career.

Your Purpose Dream Analysis will look like this:

Purpose Dreams Analysis		
GIFTS	**MATERIAL NEEDS/WANTS**	**RELATIONAL BOUNDARIES**
SWEET SPOT ANALYSIS 1. _____ 2. _____ 3. _____ 4. _____ 5. _____	Monthly Income Goal _____ Other Total Compensation Needs _____	1. _____ 2. _____ 3. _____ 4. _____ 5. _____
MOTIVATIONAL REMINDER 1. _____ 2. _____ 3. _____		
PRIORITY BUCKETS **MUSTS** 1. _____ 2. _____ 3. _____ 4. _____ 5. _____	**SHOULDS** 1. _____ 2. _____ 3. _____ 4. _____ 5. _____	**NO WAY** 1. _____ 2. _____ 3. _____ 4. _____ 5. _____

To download a free, electronic version of your Purpose Dreams Analysis, visit www.purposepromise.org/tools. If you need any assistance in compiling your analysis, please connect with a Purpose Guide. We want to make sure you have 100 percent clarity to reach your Purpose Dreams.

Compiling Your Sweet Spot Analysis

Your sweet spot is the intersection of the most important factors of your life and work. To have purpose in your work, you need to be operating in your sweet spot. When operating in your sweet spot, you will perform at high levels and have a strong impact. Your Sweet Spot Analysis will define your success qualifiers so you can go about the career-seeking process with effectiveness and efficiency.

This sweet spot is the point of intersection of three areas:

1. Your Gifts
2. Your Material Needs and Wants
3. Your Relational Boundaries

Let's further explore these three areas.

Your Gifts

The one area we have not evaluated on your career and life graph is your gifts. We are looking to identify giftedness through your passions, your talents, and your skills. These three areas make up your gifts. Passions are the things you love to do. Talents are the things you are good at naturally. Skills are things you have learned to be good at through experience.

Passions

What are the top five things you love to do?

Use the promptings below to list the top five things you love to do. Don't hesitate to go beyond five. The more detail you provide, the more awareness you will gain.

Analyze the top five highest seasons on your life graph. What were you frequently doing that you loved to do?

If you had all the time in the world and there was no material need, how would you spend your time?

When you were a kid, what did you love to do?

Talents

What are the top five things you are naturally good at?

Use the promptings below to list the top five things you are naturally good at. Don't hesitate to go beyond five. The more detail you provide, the more awareness you will gain.

Relive the top five professional accomplishments on your career graph. What do these accomplishments say about what you are naturally good at?

Think about the formal and informal positive feedback you have received throughout your career. Is there any consistency in what others told you?

When you were a kid, what did you do well?

Skills

What are the top five things you have learned to do well?

Doing specific tasks over time will develop specific skills and make you an expert at them. Much of what we do in our careers comes from skills we acquire. Use the promptings below to list the top five skills you have mastered in your life and career. Don't hesitate to go beyond five. The more detail you provide, the more awareness you will gain.

Relive the top five professional accomplishments on your career graph. What do these accomplishments say about the expertise you have gained through experience?

Do people ask you for advice about certain things? If so, this is an area in which you may be an expert.

Have you trained others on how to do something? If so, this is an area in which you may be an expert.

Through your analysis of your top passions, talents, and skills, you will most likely see some overlap. This is what we want to highlight. The gifts that will be most useful in achieving your Purpose Dreams are those that occur when you love to do something (passion) and are good at it, either naturally (talent), or through experience (skill). By identifying these intersections, you will be able to summarize your gifts and determine the type of work you are best designed to do.

Look at your top five passions, talents, and skills. Find the overlap between things you love to do and things you are good at. Distill these to discover your top five gifts.

Record them now under the heading "Gifts in the Sweet Spot Analysis" section of your Purpose Dream Analysis.

Your Material Needs and Wants

During Day Five of your Renewal Journey you clarified your material needs and wants. We started the day considering what real wealth looks like. The foundation of understanding money's relational power helped you gain this clarity. Spend a moment re-familiarizing yourself with your answers to the questions from Day Five. As you budgeted, you should now have a clearer picture of what is needed right now from a potential employer.

Your wants as well as your needs should also be considered here. They should be achievable through the progression of your career path. You budgeted what you need to start saving to accomplish your wants in two years and five years.

Record your Total Monthly Income Goal (From p. 123) under Material Needs and Wants in the Sweet Spot Analysis section of your Purpose Dream Analysis.

Beyond your monthly income, you will need to consider your total compensation needs: your benefit package, retirement plan, and any performance-based incentives. Beyond your base salary, these benefits are important to achieving your needs and wants.

Record these other compensation needs directly below your Total Monthly Income Goal.

Your Relational Boundaries

On Day Six of your Renewal Journey, you gained greater understanding of the significant relationships in your life. Healthy boundaries are keys to success in all areas of our lives. If you value something or someone (treasure) and feel called to take care of it as best you can (purpose), you should prioritize the boundaries needed to do so. Any career path you choose should have these defined boundaries present.

What boundaries are necessary in your career path to configure that relational treasure to your relational purpose?

We explored three levels of relationships: with your Creator, with yourself, and with others. When considering relational boundaries, you must start with your relationship with your Creator. Everything that matters will flow from how you prioritize your spiritual needs. Your spiritual journey will bear fruit if you give it priority. Look to the final question from yesterday (p. 119) as you determined any boundaries that could help you engage your spiritual needs.

Record these relational boundaries (from p. 123) in your Sweet Spot Analysis.

Next you must consider you. If you are not taking care of yourself, you will not be able to take care of those you cherish in your life. Analyze these questions to determine the best way to ensure health and balance in your life.

Grab Your Journal

« How many hours is optimal for you to work each week?

« How many hours do you need to rest each week?

« How many hours do you need for exercise each week?

« How many hours do you need for additional leisure to ensure your well-being?

Record these relational boundaries on your Sweet Spot Analysis now.

After you have great boundaries to take care of yourself, you are ready to define the boundaries necessary for your relationships with others. Revisit the relational boundaries that you defined on Day Six of your Renewal Journey.

Record these relational boundaries (from p. 123) on your Sweet Spot Analysis.

Your Sweet Spot Analysis is now complete. The overlap of your Gifts, your Material Needs and Wants, and the right Relational Boundaries will lead you to purpose, freedom, and the pursuit of joy!

Your Motivational Reminder

On Day Seven of your Renewal Journey, you identified healthy motivations to keep you away from temptations. There have been, are, and will continue to be many factors that will control you, as opposed to you controlling them. Family-of-origin expectations and worldly temptations can drive our purpose if we don't keep our awareness sharp. This retreat experience, however, has diminished their power over you and your career path. Revisit your Day Seven questions and answers to jot down the three temptations that can keep you from your best self, as well as ways to resist those temptations.

Record the three temptations (from p. 123) in the middle box on your Purpose Dream Analysis.

Keep them front and center to ensure that understanding reigns as you go through the N-to-Z portion of your career search.

Your Priority Buckets

Effective prioritization of your success qualifiers (gifts, needs, wants, and relational boundaries) will help you create the roadmap to a career of purpose. This prioritization will be your guide to discern which jobs and employers you should consider pursuing and where you should interview. To organize these priorities, you will create Priority Buckets.

Many of us tend to make pro/con lists when we are making an important decision. They can be helpful. Your Priority Buckets will be much more thorough. This section of your Purpose Dream Analysis will contain all the information you need to make logical decisions as you move into the N-to-Z portion of your career search. It will save you time, maximize your efficiency, and ultimately lead you to the right career choice.

Your Priority Buckets will contain the three MUST haves, the SHOULD haves, and the NO WAY (can't haves) in your career. They will help you visualize your success qualifiers.

MUSTS

What do you NEED, 100 percent, in any career path?

The answer to this question goes in your MUSTS bucket. These are the non-negotiables to identify in your career path. Every one of the MUSTS must be present in any of the careers that you are seriously considering.

The #1 MUST is your success qualifier in box 2 of your Sweet Spot Analysis: Your Monthly Income Goal and Other Total Compensation Needs.

Take that success qualifier and record it as #1 in your MUSTS priority bucket.

We recommend you get five additional success qualifiers in the MUSTS Priority Bucket based on your retreat exercises and Sweet Spot Analysis. If you have more that is OK. You should not have any fewer than six. Look back through the success qualifiers in your Sweet Spot Analysis. Determine if any of those should be considered a MUST. **If so, record it in your MUSTS bucket.**

Additionally, revisit these questions and your answers from your Renewal Journey to help you include all of your MUSTS. Pull out your career and life graph again. You have already answered these questions, but now that you have a fuller picture of your destination, answer them again:

Grab Your Journal

- « What common denominators pop out about the high points on your career graph?
- « What made you excited to get out of bed during the high points of your career?
- « If you were working within a team, how was this team constructed that made it effective? Ineffective?
- « What type of environment were you working in at the high points of your career?
- « How much autonomy/direction were you given at the high points of your career?
- « What skills, talents, or passions were you using at the high points in your career?
- « Are there any specific qualities of direct leadership that MUST be present in your direct supervisor?

Very often you can find the MUST success qualifiers at the high points on your career graph. Conversely, you may find them at the lowest points of your career graph as you determine situations you MUST avoid. Be diligent.

Record the rest of your MUSTS success qualifiers now.

SHOULDS

There are going to be some success qualifiers that you are not 100 percent sure are non-negotiables (MUSTS). If that questioning takes place, then those are most likely going to land in your SHOULDS Priority Bucket.

Not every item in the SHOULDS bucket needs to be met by a potential career opportunity. Ideally, three out of six should be met. If a possible career meets fewer than three, even if it meets all the MUSTS, that should be an indication that it's not likely to lead you to the fulfillment of your Purpose Dreams.

Many SHOULDS are revealed by analyzing the times in between the high and low points of your career.

Here are a few more questions that may prompt some SHOULDS if they are not evident:

What was my work-life balance like during the higher points of my career?

What was my work-life balance like during the lower points of my career?

What type of growth opportunity did I see during the higher points of my career?

What was I doing to develop new skills in the higher point of my career?

Record your SHOULDS success qualifiers now.

NO WAYS

The NO WAY success factors in the Priority Bucket are also non-negotiables. They cannot be present in any career path you might consider. You will often find your NO WAYS at the lowest points on your career graph.

You will want to look back at your Sweet Spot Analysis to see if any of those success factors reveal a NO WAY. Here are a few more questions to help you identify your NO WAYS:

What common denominators pop out about the low points on your career graph?

What made you dread going to work during the low points of your career?

Are there any specific qualities of direct leadership that MUST NOT be present in the direct supervisor in your career?

What type of environment were you working in at the low points of your career?

How much autonomy/direction were you given at the low points of your career?

What skills, talents, or passions were you not using at the low points in your career?

What tasks or responsibilities were prevalent during the low points in your career?

Record your NO WAYS success qualifiers now.

Once you have completed your Priority Buckets, your Purpose Dream Analysis will be complete. You are too important to settle for any career path that does not hit all of your MUSTS, most of your SHOULDS, and none of your NO WAYS.

The self-awareness gained through the Renewal Journey will lead to finding the right career suitor, being engaged, and having a joy-filled career: This is the Purpose Promise!

Does it sound too good to be true?

After completing this document, it is commonplace to wonder if that career suitor is out there. It may seem like a needle in a haystack, but that is an inaccurate assumption. The career-seeking process is like a funnel. In the beginning, when people lack awareness of their Purpose Dreams, options for employment may seem like the top of that funnel. They believe they could work at hundreds of places, in many different roles, and be happy. That mentality keeps the treadmills of disengagement running.

Through your Renewal Journey, you have gained the wisdom you need to make your way toward the bottom of the funnel. Your one-page Purpose Dream Analysis gives you the qualifiers to effectively navigate the career options before you. The process of finding the right career is so much more manageable and effective at the bottom of that funnel then at the top. Applying and committing to a few career possibilities based on your research is going to land you in the right career. In career seeking, your directed attention to the right suitor is all about quality, not quantity.

The complete Purpose Dreams Analysis is the documentation of your completion of the A-to-M. Now it is time to go through the N-to-Z portion of the career seeking process. In the back of this book, there are some general considerations for you to take your Purpose Dreams Analysis to the N-to-Z portion of your process.

We want to make sure you find purposeful employment. If you are not already connected with a Purpose Guide, connect with us at www.purposepromise.org to let us know you have completed your Purpose Dreams Analysis. We will connect with you to ensure you have an efficient strategy to connect to the right career suitor and find purposeful employment.

day TEN

The Joy Promise

So, HERE YOU ARE—DAY TEN! Today is the climax of your retreat journey. You have new, richer perspectives. You have overcome unhealthy mindsets. You have new Purpose Dreams, which will help you find your optimal career. Your commitment to this Renewal Journey has landed you close to your destination: your Purpose Promise.

Today, you will make the last day of your Renewal Journal the first day of your new pursuit! You will embark on rhythms and routines for your life that will not only let you achieve your purpose at work but help you to find sustainable joy in all areas of your life.

The First Day of Your New Pursuit

I'll never forget getting off the plane, back in Cincinnati, after my Costa Rica rainforest retreat. While I was in the rainforest, it was easy to see life's abundance, simplicity, and purpose. I had experienced a heightened sense of awareness and never wanted to return to my past status quo. But I wondered if I could sustain that level of wholeness after my retreat journey.

This is the same question you may be asking yourself now. The heightened state of awareness you have gained these last ten days is a "retreat high." It gives you the motivation to get out and implement your new-found awareness. If you don't have support or reinforcement for the discoveries you've made about yourself and your Purpose Dreams, you may get discouraged and even depressed that your outer world isn't changing as fast as you had hoped.

So, how can you sustain your "retreat high" and fulfill the promise of purpose in your career and life? You can't do it alone. We want to continue a relationship with you. Your Purpose Guide is still here to walk with you as you pursue your Purpose Dreams. We have committed to being there for you on your ten-day retreat, and we want you to continue into the next phase of your journey. We want you to continue to discern your Purpose Dreams. We want to walk with you and watch as these Purpose Dreams become a reality. We will remain committed to you for as long as you will let us be. The greatest gift you can give your Purpose Guide is to continue a relationship into the next phase of fulfilling your Purpose Dreams.

In addition to your Purpose Guide, make sure you are intentional about surrounding yourself with people who will encourage you and hold you accountable to your new Purpose Dreams. Staying in community with others who take the pursuit of purpose seriously is the only way to make that "retreat high" a way of life. We have developed a Purpose Promise learning community to help you maintain your "retreat high". Check out www.purposepromise. org/community to be a part of The Purpose Promise community. On this tenth day of your retreat, commit to making a life decision. Let the tenth day of your retreat be the rest of your life.

How do you not fall from the grace of the new-found awareness you have discovered over the last ten days?

Know that this commitment will be challenging. Old thought patterns and unhealthy messages from society are hard to conquer consistently. Living a life of purpose is a battle. You are going against the grain of the world you live in to do so.

Throughout this journey, you have gained awareness about how to enhance your life. You have liberated yourself from self-deception, and you have sought to find happiness; however, the obtaining of happiness is not the end goal. Here is the hard truth: The happiness you are feeling after the exploration of your true self is not sustainable. To have happiness become a way of life, we must focus on a shift from happiness to joy!

Happiness is a feeling. Feelings will not sustain your life's purpose. Happiness is circumstantial. Circumstances are uncontrollable. Happiness is temporary. There is more to life than the temporary fulfillment of happiness. The key to crafting a life of real purpose is the art of turning happiness into joy!

There is a peace that surpasses all understanding. Trusting and pursuing that peace will turn your happiness into joy. Seeking joy will guard your heart and mind against falling back into the lies that have plagued your past self. You were made *on* purpose *for* a purpose. Don't let life slip away as you seek a happiness that will come and go. A posture of joy will transform your mind and life!

The American Dream tells you to pursue happiness, but this is robbing you of something greater. Your Purpose Dreams allow you to sustain joy! By developing disciplines in your life that reinforce the lessons you have learned over the last ten days, you will find a lasting joy and freedom. Maintaining a contemplative awareness of owning and understanding your yesterday, today, and tomorrow will give you the foundation you need.

On retreat, joy seems omnipresent. Sustaining joy in between retreats has always been my war. To win the battles of this war, I have learned to focus on simple habits to sustain my "retreat high" and help me live out who I am called to be. Today, on your tenth day of the Renewal Journey, commit to these seven habits that will move you toward this posture of lasting joy. Your future is one of hope and purpose. Fulfillment of your purpose can only be found from this joy-filled posture.

The Inside-Out Life

When we are seeking to live life from a joy-filled posture, we do not let our external circumstances dictate our behaviors. The circumstances of our life are mostly out of our control. The one thing we can control is how we react to those circumstances. An inside-out life is more focused on our thoughts, our beliefs, our feelings, and our reactions than on external circumstances. The inside-out life takes more responsibility for what we can control and allows itself freedom from the uncontrollable. The inside-out life is not the norm, but you have the power to live it.

Contemplation is a key to living the inside-out life. Reliance on hourly, daily, monthly, and yearly retreat patterns will enable consistent contemplation. With a contemplative focus, you will have a proactive life, not a reactive life. In sports terms, think of it as playing offense, rather than defense.

The inside-out life will center on the release of your Yesterday, based on a real awareness of what it was. You will Own what was, what is, and what is to come. You will have a deeper Understanding of right perspective. Most importantly, the inside-out life will keep your personal story in proper relationship to the larger story of life. Ultimately, you are simply a character in this universal story.

Fear, shame, envy, and pride can all lead to an outside-in lifestyle. The Renewal Journey has helped you identify emotions that drive your behavior. Recognizing these emotions is the first step in controlling them. Controlling them will help you own them, which is imperative to the inside-out life.

As you reflect on the habits you want to make a regular part of your joy-filled life, be conscious of the emotions you have identified that have hindered your best self.

Grab Your Journal

« What should you do to remain living an inside-out life?

« How can you hold yourself accountable to the inside-out lifestyle?

« Do you get frustrated when circumstances dictate your emotions?

« Think about a recent experience that was not your ideal circumstance. How did you react to this circumstance?

« How could you have embraced that circumstance differently?

« What emotions arose in you as you encountered this situation?

« What could you change for the next time you experience a circumstance out of your control?

« How can you remember to change your behavior when faced with circumstances out of your control?

Remember, you do not get to choose what happens to you, but you do get to choose what happens in you when you live the inside-out life. Exploring habits that will help you live the inside-out life will significantly enhance your ability not just to be happy, but to sustain joy… I promise!

The Joy Habits
1. Live Intentionally

We've all heard the instructions: ready, aim, fire. Most Americans get this mixed up in their career search. It becomes ready, fire, aim.

They act first and calibrate later. Your courageous commitment to this Renewal Journey has set you up for success by teaching you to gain clarity of purpose before trying to find the fulfillment of that purpose. Through your wise focus on being first, you have a strong foundation to clarify your Purpose Dreams. But you are only halfway there. Now it is time to do. You were ready for change; you have aimed; now shoot for your dreams.

Defining your success qualifiers will lead to success in your career path, but during your Renewal Journey, you also discovered practices you need to do to maintain your aim and focus.

Grab Your Journal

« What routines will help you reach the Purpose Dreams you have found during your retreat time:
  « *Hourly*
  « *Daily*
  « *Monthly*
  « *Quarterly*
  « *Yearly*

Every December I go on an abbreviated Renewal Journey. I analyze my relationships and Purpose Dreams. I look back at the year and determine where I need to change, celebrate what has taken place, and plan the year ahead. Set an intention to develop rhythms in your life.

Only one thing will create immeasurable joy in your life, and that is understanding of and obedience to your purpose. Your Purpose Dreams themselves hold no power without the action to reach those dreams. Reaching your dreams takes serious work. Intentionality is the ongoing mental focus to get you there.

2. Receive

Being generous is a great way to remain joyful. Being generous brings joy into others' lives and, consequently, into our lives. Receiving generosity from others comes less naturally to most of us, but it's no less important in a joy-filled life.

I am a poor receiver. I do not receive well because deep down it makes me feel dependent. This has been an issue I have had to work through. My wife giggles every time I stumble through the garage door with every grocery bag on my shoulder. I grunt my way toward the kitchen as if I am proving in a world's strongest man competition. She will always ask me if I need a hand, but she knows I'll say no. Somewhere along the line, I imagined that a real man can bring in all the groceries in one trip.

I have to cultivate an intentional habit of receiving help, gifts, quality time, or acts of service. I have learned that receiving these gifts from others is often a gift to them. If giving is better than receiving, then every time I receive a gift I am giving another person the gift of giving. With that awareness, I have become better at receiving, as I have understood the blessing in being blessed.

Ingrained in the difficulty we have with receiving is the lie that we can do life alone. As we broke down the four levels of wealth and celebrated our relational treasures on our retreat, we remembered that we are built to do life in relationship. My independence can keep me aware of how I am designed to be reliant on others. When I receive, I become more relationally wealthy.

When I hear any of the following words, I need to stop and recognize my default setting of independence. By recognizing these cues, I can be more disciplined to receive.

How can I pray for you?

Can I help you…?

I'll pay for that.

Can I lend a hand with that?

How about if I do…?

These are just a few of the common phrases I hear when others in my life genuinely show they want to help. If receiving is a struggle for you, tune your ears to these phrases so you can develop a habit of receiving.

There is a humility that comes from receiving from others. Pride brings forth disgrace, while humility brings forth wisdom. The joy-filled life is full of receiving and giving freely.

> **Grab Your Journal**
>
> « Do you have a hard time receiving?
>
> « If so, why?
>
> « Can you think of a situation in which you felt helpless to help others you loved?
>
> « Would it have been a gift to be able to help them in that situation?
>
> « How do you feel when you give to others?
>
> « How do others react to you when you allow them to give to you?

3. Embrace Hardship

Committing to a joy-filled life does not mean you will no longer experience hardships. Pain, hurt, theft, destruction, and death are just some of the negative things that will still come your way. They will not be easy, but with the right posture toward these difficulties you will overcome them.

As you looked over your life and career graphs this week, some of the lower points ended up being your best teaching circumstances. When we realize that adversity leads to resilience and that resilience creates character, we can look at hardship through a new lens. Hardship can advance our purpose if understood from the right perspective.

Sometimes it might seem as though life is going against you. No matter what you do, nothing seems to go the way you expect it to. To live a joy-filled life, you must be adaptable in these seasons of life. Change is constant. The rapid pace of change can be daunting these days. How you adapt to the ever-changing external pressures of our world is essential to living a joy-filled life.

How do you maintain a habit of finding joy in adversity? When it is dark and you are trying to navigate through the darkness, what do you do? You seek light. Gratitude is the switch that turns on the light in our world when adversity strikes. I know it seems counter-intuitive, but when you are in a season of adversity, return to the exercises you completed on Day Four of your retreat. Take inventory of your great gifts, and you will start to ooze gratitude. The shift in mindset from focusing on the adversity to rejoicing in your gifts will give you strength to fight through.

You may be in a season of prosperity. If that is the case, give thanks, but don't get bitter if that season changes. You may be in a season of hardship. If that is the case, be resilient as more fruitful days lie ahead. Whatever season you find yourself in, adapt where you need to, but keep right perspective: Life is full of different seasons. You can't always take control of the season you are in, but you can control how you react to it.

> **Grab Your Journal**
>
> « How could the way you embrace hardship teach your loved ones about character?
> « Look back at the lower points of your life and career graph.
> « How did you handle adversity in those seasons?
> « How were your eyes opened to right perspective in those seasons?
> « Is adapting to change hard for you?
> « What is one practical way you can enact gratitude when you are in a season of adversity?

4. Reduce Noise

So much more of life is caught than taught. We learn so much about ourselves and the life around us from what we take in. It is difficult not to get caught up in the external affairs of our world. This Ten-day Renewal Journey has given you many examples of lies you believed that were not based on you. On this retreat you have reduced the noise of this world. Being aware of the world's messages and their power is a discipline that will help you to sustain joy.

The world's marketing messages are not necessarily for your benefit. Be conscious of what you are taking in. What we consume will drive much of our thought. Make wise decisions about what you let enter your mind and heart. The messages can be quite subtle. Learn to be aware of what is hidden beneath the surface.

Grab Your Journal

« What media outlets do you enjoy?

« Are they based in truth?

« Are they healthy for you?

« Are they positive?

« When making decisions about the music you listen to, do you consider its message?

« When making decisions about what you watch, do you consider its message?

« When making decisions about where you get your news, do you consider its message?

Over the last ten days, you have gained the right perspective about yourself. Do not fall prey to who the world wants you to be. Be intentional about reducing unnecessary noise in your life.

5. Retreat to Renew

On the Renewal Journey you have been analyzing your mindsets. Your mind had power over your beliefs and actions, but as you have taken control of those mindsets, you have gained freedom. The mind can be a battlefield that keeps us from our best selves. By taking captive the mindsets that enslaved you, you have renewed your mind!

The renewed mind has right understanding. This is the product of retreating to find self-awareness. The right understanding you have gained through these ten days has been an outpouring of your dedication to establishing better purpose.

The renewed mind operates on wisdom, not knowledge. The wisdom of a renewed mind realizes you are not at the center of life. Worldly knowledge puts you at the center of everything and tells you to do what is best for you. This perspective leads to the outside-in life that will lead to short-term temptation, shallow relationships, and a lack of purpose. The inside-out life allows you to be proactive about life. By retreating you have renewed your mind and empowered the inside-out life that sustains joy.

The renewed mind is on guard against lies of the outside world. The lies that we believe can hold our best self prisoner to our best self. The renewed mind sustains your real truth.

The renewed mind is graceful, not judgmental. In an outside-in life, you will blame others for your hardships. You can't control others, so the inside-out life will help you coexist with them without judging or wishing them ill. Focus on you and how you react; you will experience joy as you renew your mind no matter what the circumstances.

The renewed mind releases control. Control is only useful when you are in a controlled environment, but this world is not a controlled environment. The renewed mind knows that you can't control life.

Renewing your mind is an acquired skill. Retreating is the habit that leads to the renewing of your mind. Do not let this retreat be a one-time event. Let the retreat experience propel you to make retreating a habit so you can pursue purpose, freedom, and joy!

Your Renewal Journey has given you your true self. Losing that self to the dreams of the world is no longer an option. Your Purpose Dreams are a gift. What you do with that gift is now up to you. Retreating regularly to renew your mind will ensure your Purpose Dreams become your Purpose Reality!

> **Grab Your Journal**
>
> « What disciplines can you add to your day to help you slow down and live an inside-out life with the right perspective?
>
> « How can you more effectively recognize lies that the world is telling you about yourself?
>
> « What habits of retreating to renew are you going to take?

The Purpose Dreams you have today may change through the different seasons of your life. The only way to be proactive in anticipating them is to retreat to renew.

6. The Next Journey: Let Joy Be Your Strength

It has been an honor to be your guide throughout this journey. Stay connected with your Purpose Guide as life changes. We are here to encourage and help you find a rhythm that works for you as you live out your Renewal Journey. The continued discipline of renewal will develop an abundant life. Retreating (BE) coupled with sustainable habits (DO) leads to joy.

A life of joy will give you strength. You will need this strength. It is not *if* you will face adversity, but *when*. Strength prepares you to live in peace knowing that the difficulties of life cannot rob you of true joy!

Continue to pursue your unique and wonderful self and enjoy the Real Dream: abundant purpose, freedom, and joy!

Today is the tenth day of your Renewal Journey retreat. This tenth day is the rest of your life.

BE YOU and DO JOY!

The A-to-Z

BARRY HAS BECOME A GOOD FRIEND. He and I first met about eighteen months ago when he was on a networking journey to find the right career. He had been downsized and was a senior-level manager. The job market was not favorable to senior-level managers here, so he had many ups and downs on his long journey.

I was his 113th networking meeting. He ended up having over 130 networking meetings. That is not a typo. He had 130 networking meetings before he found his new career. The focal point of most of those meetings was on the N-to-Z, but near the end, Barry took a different approach. He stepped back and defined his success qualifiers by engaging an A-to-M approach. The individual awareness of his Purpose Dreams made all the difference in how managed his N-to-Z more effectively.

That was an exhausting season for Barry. It was fruitful on some fronts, as he made many new and genuine friendships, but overall it was an inefficient process of finding his ideal career. Barry is a very self-aware guy, but he is a doer. His propensity was to get out and find that new job as fast as he could. It is commonplace for career seekers to engage in the N-to-Z ambitiously, just as Barry did; however, without individual awareness and declaration of success qualifiers, the career seeker is not equipped to do the N-to-Z efficiently.

I have great news for you: You will not need to buy 130 cups of coffee in your N-to-Z quest. Now that you have your Purpose Dream Analysis, you have the individual awareness to be efficient in your pursuit of the perfect career. You know who you are; you know what you need and what you want. With your Purpose Dream Analysis you will be able to:

« Build your resumé based on your highlighted accomplishments on your career graph.

« Seek actively hiring employers who are good career suitors based on all of your MUSTS, most of your SHOULDS, and none of your NO WAYS. This ensures you will be operating in your sweet spot of gifts, needs, and wants.

« Seek employers that you have identified that are in line with all your needs and wants. These employers may or may not be hiring, but with a wise methodology on building a relationship with them and staying top of mind, you could create your dream position.

« Leverage your network wisely. Your network should be your greatest asset among your N-to-Z efforts, but that is only the case if you are intentional about the methodology.

« Network effectively and efficiently with concise communication of who you are and the sweet spot you are seeking to fulfill your Purpose Dreams.

« Interview with a clear awareness of who you are, where your sweet spot is, and how that has benefited your previous employers.

« Interview potential employers about their likelihood to fulfill your needs and wants in the short- and long-term career goals.

« Negotiate employment offers that meet your needs and wants from the outset.

« Engage in all career seeking N-to-Z activities with purpose, based on your Purpose Dreams.

Career counselors widely communicate N-to-Z best practices. There is some good advice and some not-so-good advice out there. It is not the purpose of this book to detail the best practices of N-to-Z, but one thing is for sure: The A-to-M is the key to unlocking efficiency amidst the N-to-Z. You have the competitive advantage in the career-seeking market with the A-to-M. You are prepped to do the N-to-Z. Now that you have done the A-to-M, your A to Z will conclude with the right career to fulfill your Purpose Dreams.

Please continue to walk with you Purpose Guide during the N-to-Z. Your Guide can help you manage the process. Collectively, we have helped thousands of career seekers obtain their Purpose Dream. Your Purpose Guide was your retreat guide through the A-to-M and is also your guide through the N-to-Z. Doing the N-to-Z alone can be a real challenge, even with a well-developed Purpose Dream Analysis. We are here to help and are grateful to fulfill the process with you and see your Purpose Dreams matched with the ideal career suitor.

If you are having trouble with the steps to navigate the N-to-Z, we are just a click away: www.purposepromise.org

You will not conquer the most difficult journeys in life in isolation!

The Purpose Promise was founded to guide you, the purpose seeker, on a journey toward a richer life. We are equipped and excited to take the journey with you.

We are a proven, non-judgmental resource to get your Purpose Dreams activated.

Purposeful employment will not find YOU. You must claim it.

Visit us at:

purposepromise.org

to interact with your Purpose Guide and find your purpose.

Work should be one of the greatest parts of your life! Our Mission is to help disengaged workers change their view of work and to guide them in the journey to find their unique purpose. If this mission inspires you, you could become a certified Purpose Promise Guide.

Becoming a certified Purpose Guide equips you with the tools to walk with disengaged workers to help them obtain their Purpose Dreams. Being a certified Guide is fruitful and rewarding employment. We would love to have you join our team. Visit us at purposepromise.org/guides to learn more about how to change lives by being a catalyst in the Purpose Promise Movement.

John McCarthy
Founder and President of The Purpose Promise Movement
Author, Speaker, and Purpose Guide

About the Author

John McCarthy is a visionary entrepreneur working to disrupt the status quo of how people look at success. John established his first nonprofit while in college to help students further their self-awareness through retreat. Since then, his passion is to disciple individuals toward discovering how they are made, who made them, and how to find purpose at work and in life.

At age 24, John launched AGI Management, a recruitment firm focused on changing the landscape of the hospitality industry (an industry noted for turnover) by placing great managers with only great employers. AGI Management uses a counter-intuitive methodology of recruiting managers by encouraging them to gain self-awareness prior to changing careers.

Through the 15 years of growing AGI Management, John developed a passion for walking with job seekers toward a more thorough career-seeking process. John embraces the urgency to curb the disengaged workforce in America. John's leadership and expertise have equipped him with a platform to change the paradigm of how Americans look at work. Find out more at purposepromise.org.

John, his wife, and their three awesome children reside in Cincinnati where they enjoy having fun, investing in the community, playing sports, participating in local theatre, and making new friends.